Sacred Grammar

Sacred Grammar

James Wilson Beaty, PhD

Copyright © 2011 by James Wilson Beaty, PhD.

Library of Congress Control Number: 2010914295
ISBN: Hardcover   978-1-4535-8567-2
              Softcover   978-1-4535-8566-5

All rights reserved. No part of this book may be reproduced or transmitted in any form or by any means, electronic or mechanical, including photocopying, recording, or by any information storage and retrieval system, without permission in writing from the copyright owner.

This book was printed in the United States of America.

To order additional copies of this book, contact:
Xlibris Corporation
1-888-795-4274
www.Xlibris.com
Orders@Xlibris.com
24166

Contents

Introduction 11

Chapter One: The Eight Parts of Speech 15
Chapter Two: The Case for the Three Cases 24
Chapter Three: The Simple Sentence 36
Chapter Four: The Complex Sentence.....................................43
Chapter Five: The Compound Sentence..................................57
Chapter Six: The Compound-Complex Sentence 71
Chapter Seven: Decorating Sentences....................................78
Chapter Eight: Verbs, Nouns' Best Friends 92
Chapter Nine: A Moment with Verbals 130
Chapter Ten: The Comma 143
Chapter Eleven: Writing That Paper....................................164

Epilogue 185
Appendix..187
Works Cited 215
Index..217
Scripture Index..223

Dedication

This book is dedicated to my father, Walter Kirkpatrick Beaty, Sr., whose impeccable grammar captured and held my attention.

ACKNOWLEDGEMENT

I acknowledge my students at Beulah Heights University who taught me more than I taught them. SACRED GRAMMAR would not have happened without the editing of Frank Beaty and the support of Anita Beaty.

INTRODUCTION

I know of no way to correct incorrect speaking or incorrect writing without putting into practice the rules of grammar. I came to this conclusion by trial and error—my trials and my students' errors! Eventually I learned that students can avoid the frustrations of writing (and help teachers avoid much of the frustration of grading papers) by carefully examining sentence structure. Together we check errors, and together we applaud correctness. I began years ago developing this process in an American literature class.

One day, after returning student papers, I dismissed class and walked to my office. When I got there I noticed that a student in the class had followed me. He had received a grade of B, but he was visibly upset. I had noted comma splices and other grammatical errors. The polite young man had no problem with his grade; he wanted an explanation of my comments in the margins of his paper. As I explained my notations, he listened intently. When I showed him commas placed between independent clauses, he stopped me. He said, "Dr. Beaty, I'm an English major, and I'm not sure what you mean by an independent clause. And I'm not certain about comma splices." I explained the difference between independent and dependent clauses. I showed him that a semicolon in place of a comma between two independent clauses corrects the comma splice. I told him that a comma and a coordinate conjunction (such as *and* or *but*) between two independent clauses is another way to punctuate the compound sentence. He stopped me again. He exclaimed that he didn't know "a compound from a dog pound!" He told me that he never uses semicolons (;) because he feels uneasy, not knowing when they are correct.

Please get this picture. Here sat with me a third-year English major in a state university who hoped to teach English in the public schools.

Yet, he stated that this was the first time anyone had asked him to learn the structural elements of the sentence. I learned, to my dismay, that this young man was not the exception; he was the rule. I learned later that very few of his classmates could identify compound sentences.

Studying the structure of a house reveals how the house is built. Why must we place a certain brick, beam or wall exactly where we do? Studying the structure of a sentence shows the same thing. It makes clear how the sentence is built, but more importantly, it tells *why it* must be built that way. The eight parts of speech are the building blocks of clauses, and clauses are the building blocks of sentences. If someone says, "I seen him when he done it," most of us hear the errors. But how many of us know the grammatical reasons why "I saw him when he did it" is correct? Only the rules of grammar give those answers.

Therefore we begin *Sacred Grammar* with the eight parts of speech. An examination of clauses follows, and from there we move on to the four kinds of sentences and how to punctuate them according to their structure. Finally, after we have tackled the sentence, we will look at the paragraph and then at writing the paper.

Sacred Grammar will chart a course for people just learning to write a composition. It will assist the more advanced writer who still finds the task difficult. This book teaches the basics and takes both instructor and student beyond the basics into less stressful writing. Confident editing will follow as the knowledge of grammar gives the ability to correct and improve what has been composed in the first draft.

The Bible for Grammar?

The Bible is not a grammar textbook. But I know of no other book better suited to teach grammar and composition. Generations of children have learned to read with the Bible as their primer. Schools today that put little emphasis on writing could benefit from using the Bible as a model. Mastering proper usage and learning spiritual truths at the same time sweeten these endeavors.

Take this guide and go through it. Complete each self-quiz. Practice makes perfect almost every time. Consult *Sacred Grammar* whenever you have to write a paper or whenever you need to edit what you have written.

Answers for the self-quizzes appear in the appendix. Check your answers with your instructor. Early exercises in this book will ask you to write. Be sure to consult your instructor whenever possible.

Paul the Apostle, in 1 Corinthians 14:40, asks that we do all things decently and in order. The New International Version (NIV) translates this verse beautifully: "But everything should be done in a fitting and orderly way." This is good advice for writers. We should add another verse that urges "to study to show yourself approved of God, a workman who needs not to be ashamed, rightly dividing the word of truth" (2 Tim. 2:15). The word *study* in this verse comes from the Greek word *spoudason*, which translates, "be diligent." Let us follow this command in our effort to master the language. The fact that you are reading these words indicates that you want to improve your writing skills. A genuine desire to write well and to speak correctly is half the battle; *Sacred Grammar* will prove indispensable for the other half.

From Frustration to Satisfaction

I recall one student's experience that changed his attitude toward writing. Early in a semester years ago, I assigned an essay to be written on any subject of personal interest. I wanted a writing sample from each student. The class was English 101, freshman English, at a state university. I asked that each essay include a thesis statement with a conclusion that supported the thesis. A young man, not at all pleased with the assignment, spoke with me after class. He said he couldn't think of a topic. I asked what interested him.

As we walked to my office, he gave an answer that I have not forgotten. "I ain't interested in nothing," he said.

I was taken aback. *Surely*, I thought, *this young man has some interests that he can recall and share on paper*. He and I sat in silence for moments that seemed a long time. Finally, I spoke, "What are you doing this weekend?"

"Nothing," he answered glumly. And without hesitation he asked me, "What are you doing this weekend?"

I explained that I was going to Daytona to the races, the Busch Chase on Saturday and the Daytona 500 the following day. I asked, "Do you like NASCAR racing?"

"Like it?" he brightened. "I love it. Richard Petty is my favorite driver!"

Enter Richard Petty, Car Number 43

We talked about auto racing, and within minutes I had become a fellow race fan instead of a dull English professor. I had touched on a topic that charged this fellow's battery. Before leaving my office, he had decided to write his four-hundred-word essay on the popular racer, Richard Petty. This young man was not the least impressed with my credentials as a university professor; however, my knowledge of the famous number 43, the details of the Petty car and my familiarity with the racing family won him.

A week later after a few conferences with me and several visits to the writing center, he submitted an interesting paper explaining how Richard Petty had come into fame and fortune as a race driver. The paper became attractive proportionately to the writer's response to the subject matter. The research material he found fascinated him, and his vitality reached the written page. His success followed specific steps from start to finish. He followed a plan. He did not sit down without careful preparation to begin writing about Richard Petty. Many of my students face the blank screen without any prewriting or preparation. That's nothing short of self-torture and a blueprint for failure. In its final lessons, *Sacred Grammar* will guide you through the preparation and the writing of the composition.

ONE

The Eight Parts of Speech

Why Know a Word's Part of Speech?

Recently, a professional athlete in a postgame interview said, "We won the game because the whole team played *good*." We hear this kind of error all the time. Ask someone, "How are you doing?" Often the answer comes, "I'm doing *good*." A sportscaster, speaking of the stamina of right-handed Atlanta Braves pitcher John Smoltz, said, "He could have *went* three more innings." Another announcer offered, "Nobody would *have gave* him much of a chance to come back at all!" Last year I attended the graduation ceremony at a prominent Atlanta high school, and I overheard a graduate introduce his friend to his parents, saying to them, "*Me* and *him* graduated together from middle school too." I heard a man in a coffee shop say to the clerk, "I painted with a guy today, and I didn't know that *him* and you are roommates." Many people speak this way these days, even educated folks. Pointing out these errors is never intended to shame or judge anyone. Correctness is valuable, of course, but learning *why* a sentence is correct or incorrect is essential, empowering us to speak and to write clearly, with confidence, for the rest of our lives. Our procedure in *Sacred Grammar* therefore begins with the eight parts of speech.

A word's part of speech is determined by its function in a sentence. Consider the word *last*. The synoptic Gospels, Matthew, Mark and Luke, teach us the following:

> The first shall be last, and the last shall be first.

In this sentence, the word *last* appears twice. The first *last* is an adjective describing the subject *first*. The second *last* functions as a noun, the subject of the verb *shall be*. Judges 14:17 states that some festivals *last* as long as seven days. So we see that the word *last* in these three instances functions as an adjective, a noun and a verb! Good writing follows an understanding of how the parts of speech work together.

The Eight Parts of Speech List

The first time I heard the parts of speech explained, my ninth grade English teacher stood in front of the class and listed eight words, vertically, down the left side of the blackboard. She asked our bored, sleepy class to learn, by next day, the names and definitions of the eight parts of speech. Watching her list them was not exciting, but it was a good start. She was a fine teacher, God rest her, and she was doing what I wish more teachers were doing today. She was attempting to teach grammar beginning with the good old-fashioned eight parts of speech. Knowing and understanding the parts of speech is the first giant step toward the goal of writing correctly.

NOUN. A noun is a word that names a person, a place or a thing. Note that all dictionaries list the word, its pronunciation and its part of speech with an abbreviated letter or letters. I am looking at the word *air* in the *Webster's New Universal Unabridged Dictionary*. It lists *air*, [ar] as its pronunciation, n. as the part of speech most frequently used, followed by twenty-three definitions of the word as a noun. The listings under *air* in this dictionary go on to show how *air* functions as several other parts of speech. I have chosen the word *air* to show that an intangible substance can be a noun, a thing. Some of my students argue with Mr. Webster at this point, believing *air* not to be a thing, a noun. They lose this argument every time. A perfect example of an intangible substance occurs with the use of the word *air* in the following verse:

> So they took soot from a furnace and stood before Pharaoh. Moses tossed it into the **air**, and festering boils broke out on men and animals. (Exod. 9:10)

Ideally, each time you read or write anything, a good dictionary should be available. Bible study is impossible without a Bible. Responsible writing is impossible without a dictionary. Note that the words typed in **bold** letters in 2 Samuel 18:18b are nouns, naming persons, places or things:

> I have no **son** to carry on the **memory** of my **name.** He named the **pillar** after himself, and it is called **Absalom's Monument** to this **day**.

Because of limited space, I'll not list any more nouns from the Bible. I must say, however, that the writer of Hebrews 4 fascinates the reader with a repetition of some form of the word *rest*. Why don't you *rest* a moment and count the *rest* of the number of times *rest* appears in that *rest*ful chapter. Novelist Charles Dickens in many of his novels thrills his readers with conscious repetition. In the first paragraph of *Little Dorrit*, Dickens uses some form of the word *stare* ten times to capture the suffocating heat of a Marseilles afternoon.

PRONOUN. A pronoun is a word that takes the place of a noun to avoid needless repetition of the noun itself. Words such as *anyone, he, her, him, it, our, she, that, their, them, themselves, us, we, what, whatever, who, whom, which, you, yours* and *yourself* are all pronouns. Each of these words takes the place of a noun, singular or plural.

Note that the words in **bold** type in 2 Samuel 18:33 are all pronouns and refer to King David or his dead son, Absalom:

> The king was shaken. **He** went up to the room over the gateway and wept. As **he** went, **he** said: O **my** son Absalom! **My** son, **my** son Absalom! If only **I** had died instead of **you**—O Absalom, **my** son, **my** son!"

Note please that the possessive pronoun *my* in this verse functions as an adjective modifying the noun, *son*.

What Are Pronoun Antecedents?

One cardinal rule states that every pronoun in formal, written English must have a clear antecedent, an earlier word to which it refers. That antecedent will be a noun or a pronoun. It can also be a phrase or a clause appearing earlier in the sentence. Every pronoun must have a clear antecedent, and the pronoun must agree in number (singular or plural) with its antecedent. All pronouns take the places of nouns, and the noun is the antecedent. The words *you yourselves have seen* in Exodus 19:4 tell the reader that, *you*, the descendents, the children of Israel, have witnessed an event. The rest of Exodus 19:4 reads,

> What I did to Egypt, and how I carried you on eagles' wings and brought you unto myself.

Remember that whenever a pronoun appears in written or spoken English, it must have a clear antecedent that agrees in number (singular or plural) with the pronoun. In Exodus 19:3 the word *descendents* is the plural antecedent of the plural pronoun *you* that begins verse 4.

ADJECTIVE. An adjective is a word that describes a noun or a pronoun. I cannot emphasize enough the fact that adjectives describe *only* nouns and pronouns. Study the following sentence: *She is a good singer*. This sentence is correct because *good*, an adjective, modifies the noun *singer*. If I write *She sings good*, I have misused the adjective *good* to describe the verb *sings*. This is a no-no! Adjectives describe *only* nouns and pronouns, no other parts of speech, not now, not ever, never. Note that the words in **bold** type in 2 Samuel 19:32a are adjectives describing nouns that follow them:

> Now Barzillai was a very **old** man, **eighty** years of age.

VERB. A verb is a word that expresses an action or a state of being. Note that the **bold** words in 1 Kings 3:1a are action verbs:

> Solomon **made** an alliance with Pharaoh king of Egypt and **married** his daughter.

Note that the word in **bold** letters in 2 Kings 5:1a is a state of being verb:

> Now Naaman **was** commander of the army of the king of Aram.

ADVERB. An adverb is a word that describes a verb, an adjective or another adverb. Look at the arrows in the parts of speech chart that point from the adverb to the verb, the adjective and back to the adverb. Note that the word in **bold** letters in Acts 17:16 is an adverb that describes the verb *was distressed*:

> While Paul was waiting for them in Athens, he was **greatly** distressed to see that the city was full of idols.

PREPOSITION. A preposition is simply a word that joins its object to the rest of the sentence. Note that the words in **bold** type in the following verse are prepositions forming prepositional phrases that join their objects to the rest of the sentence:

> For he chose us **in** him **before** the creation **of** the world to be holy and blameless **in** his sight. (Eph. 1:3)

Grammar books define a preposition in various ways. All those definitions are good; however, I have found that, over the years, students understand readily that the preposition first and foremost joins its object to the rest of the sentence. This "object word" following its preposition forms the often written prepositional phrase.

CONJUNCTION. A conjunction is a word that joins words to each other or groups of words to each other. Note that the words in **bold** type in 2 Timothy 4:6 are conjunctions:

> **For** I am already being poured out like a drink offering, **and** the time has come for my departure.

Both are conjunctions whose names we will learn later.

INTERJECTION. An interjection is a word or a group of words that exclaim a strong feeling. The expressions *Wow! Ouch! Glory to God!* are all interjections, usually punctuated with the exclamation point (!).

Sometimes an interjection can be formed by several words, even a clause. Notice that the interjection is the only one of the eight parts of speech that functions on its own. It does not interact with any other part of speech. Note that the words in **bold** type in Mark 11:21 form interjections that feature exclamation points:

Peter remembered and said to Jesus, "**Rabbi, look! The fig tree that you cursed has withered!**"

Listing and learning the eight parts of speech is a good start toward understanding the sentence, but memorizing definitions is not enough. The following chart examines the eight parts of speech horizontally as we read and write them across the page. Because parts of speech in and of themselves are so deadly dull and downright boring, I devised this *horizontal* chart to alleviate the sleepiness of what I call the *vertical* approach to learning the eight parts of speech.

The Eight Parts of Speech Chart

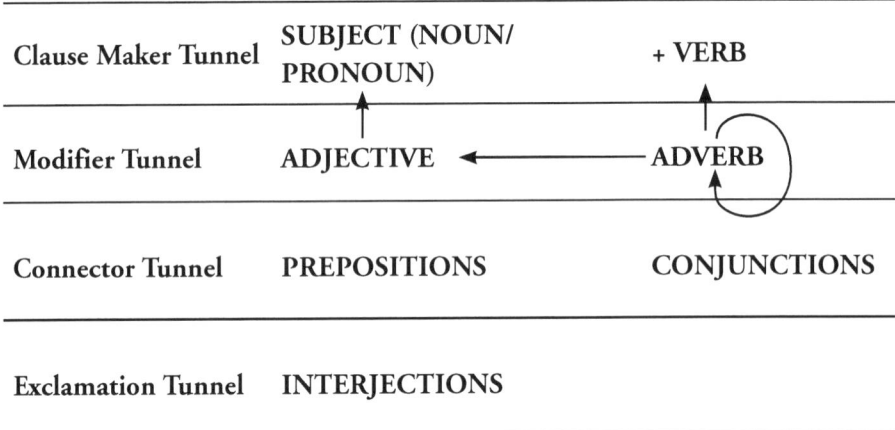

The *horizontal* approach shows that all parts of speech interact with each other in clauses or phrases. The only exception is the eighth part of speech, the interjection. Note please that a noun or a pronoun *subject* joins a verb to form a clause. I refer to this joining as the subject-verb cluster. We will explore the clause in the next chapter. Review these eight parts of speech until you know them cold. Put them on flash cards with definitions and examples on the flip side.

Coordinate Conjunctions: FANBOYS

Also, be sure to make flash cards for the lists of the different categories within a part of speech. For example, write seven coordinate conjunctions: *for, and, nor, but, or, yet* and *so*. Some important subordinate conjunctions that must be written on flash cards are as follows: *after, as, as if, because, before, if, since, unless, until, when, where, whether* and *while*. We will add other subordinate conjunctions when we focus on dependent clauses.

Let's take this opportunity to put the Parts of Speech Chart into action. Genesis 1:1 states,

> In the beginning God created the heavens and the earth.

Note how every word in this first sentence of the Bible fits with every other word. Listen to the harmony. All words of all correctly written sentences in English do the same. If each word or group of words fits correctly, a clearly measured sentence results. *In the beginning* is a prepositional phrase. It is a phrase, not a clause, because it forms a group of related words that does *not* contain a subject (noun or pronoun) and verb. *In the beginning* could never be a clause because there is no subject-verb cluster. Before we examine grammatically the rest of Genesis 1:1, let us take a break in order to note a famous man's playful bantering with the part of speech we call the preposition.

England's prime minister, Sir Winston Churchill, fond of his own writing style and reportedly criticized for his use of a preposition at the end of a sentence, defended himself and illustrated the silliness of hyper-adherence to rules by exclaiming, "This is the sort of nonsense UP with which I will not put." He made his point well, as we can see in his intentionally awkward sentence. However, ending a sentence with a preposition is risky business. Seasoned writers do it on occasion, but they are taking license when they do so. Writing teachers say that a preposition is a word that joins its object to the rest of the sentence. Therefore, those of us struggling to improve our writing skills avoid ending a sentence with a preposition. Note that the words in **bold** type in Jeremiah 26:9b are prepositions that join their objects to the rest of the sentence:

> And all the people crowded **around** Jeremiah **in** the house **of** the Lord.

Let me reiterate that the preposition is a word that joins its object to the rest of the sentence. Remember that the total number of words in prepositional phrases comprises a high percentage of the total number of words in sentences. This is no big deal; however, it is worth noting that prepositional phrases taken away from the sentence leave only the skeleton of the sentence. Knowing this fact makes for easy editing. Making editing easier is a big deal.

Let's go back to Genesis 1:1a:

In the beginning God created the heavens and the earth.

The word that expresses an act or action is *created*. After locating the verb we find the subject or the word that tells who or what is doing the *creating*. Suppose we were tempted to say that *beginning* is the verb. If we know that *in the beginning* is a prepositional phrase, it follows that *beginning* is the object of the preposition *in*. The object of a preposition cannot be the subject of a verb because it already functions as the object of the preposition. No word at the same time can be both an object and a subject. The Parts of Speech Chart comes into play in analyzing grammatically the first sentence of the Bible. The word *God* names the one doing the acting. The words *God created* form this subject-verb cluster, the first clause in the Bible. Later, when we decorate sentences (chapter seven), we will learn other marks for subjects, verbs and objects. The nouns *heavens* and *earth* are both direct objects in this first sentence as they are the words that answer the question, *created* what? These words indicate the receiving of the action of the verb. Learn and write on a flash card that direct objects receive the action of the action verb. Time and again we will look back to the Parts of Speech Chart for the composing of sentences and for editing.

Points to Review

- Define the clause
- Make 3 × 5 flash cards in order to review
- The function of the word in the sentence (its relationship to other words in the sentence) determines its part of speech
- Adjectives describe *only* nouns and pronouns
- Adverbs describe *only* verbs, adjectives and other adverbs

- Memorize the Parts of Speech Chart
- Learn the most frequent comma splice error
- Subject-verb agreement
- Define each of the eight parts of speech
- The importance of a good dictionary
- The vertical and horizontal approaches of the parts of speech
- Seven coordinate conjunctions
- A dozen subordinate conjunctions
- Sir Winston Churchill and the preposition
- Define the simple sentence

Self-quiz for Chapter One: The Eight Parts of Speech

1. Define a clause.
2. Define a phrase.
3. What determines a word's part of speech in a sentence?
4. Define a simple sentence.
5. Sir Winston said what about prepositions?
6. List seven coordinate conjunctions.
7. List twelve subordinate conjunctions.
8. List ten prepositions.
9. Define a preposition.
10. Name the most frequently used type of phrase in English.
11. What is the most frequent comma splice error?

Writing Exercises for Chapter One: The Eight Parts of Speech

1. Write five simple sentences and underline each subject with one line and each complete verb with two lines.
2. Write a brief paragraph that explains the vertical and horizontal approaches to learning the eight parts of speech. In each sentence underline each subject with one line and each verb with two lines. Place [brackets] around each complete clause. Note: This is the beginning of our decorating sentences. We will address decoration in a later chapter.

TWO

The Case for the Three Cases

Now that we have touched upon the eight parts of speech and how they help build a clause, let us move to the three cases. I remember some of my students' answers when I asked them to name the three cases in English. For fun they answered "pillowcase," "suitcase" and "nutcase." The *Hodges' Harbrace Handbook*, fifteenth edition, page 775, gives a better definition: *Case* is the form of a noun or pronoun that indicates the relationship of the noun or pronoun to other words in a sentence. Nouns and pronouns can be subjects or subject complements (subjective case), objects (objective case) or markers of possession (possessive case).

This highfalutin definition is correct and excellent for grammar texts. But what does it mean? More simply put, English nouns and pronouns come in three possible forms (cases). These forms are determined by how these nouns or pronouns are being used in a particular sentence. The three cases are subjective, objective and possessive.

As you might notice, except for the possessive case for nouns (which we will cover shortly), only pronouns change form according to their particular case in a sentence. For instance, Colossians 2:15 reads,

> And having disarmed the powers and authorities, he made
> a public spectacle of them, triumphing over them by the
> cross.

This sentence, written by St. Paul, contains three pronouns: *he* (subjective case), *them* (objective case) and, once again, *them* (objective case). It's just that easy. Why not *him*, *they* and *they*? Because no one wants to say "*him* made a public spectacle," or "triumphing over *they*." It would sound crazy. However, we must go beyond sound and learn why those expressions are incorrect. "*Me* and *him* competed for the starting position." This sentence was spoken in a nationally televised interview by a student athlete at a state university in the United States of America. I regret to tell you that my ears heard that statement. Woe is me! There is a case for the three cases. Neither *me* nor *him* can serve as a subject of a verb. These two pronouns are always in the objective case, objects of something.

Hodges' Harbrace Handbook, fifteenth edition, page 90, is helpful in this matter: "It can be useful to think in terms of territories to distinguish the subjective and objective cases. That is, the part of a sentence before the verb is 'subject territory' and pronouns in that position appear in the subjective case. The rest of the sentence is 'object territory,' and pronouns in that part of the sentence almost always appear in the objective form. The only exception occurs when the verb is a form of *to be*." Since the pronoun *they* is the subjective case form, it cannot be used as an object. And since the pronoun *them* is the objective case form, it cannot be used as a subject. The pronoun *their* is the possessive case form that indicates ownership.

For now let's set aside nouns as far as case is concerned. Words that name persons, places or things change form only when they become plural or when they are in the possessive case, indicating ownership, as in Acts 5:15b:

> People brought the sick into the streets and laid them on beds and mats so that at least Peter's shadow might fall on some of them as he passed by.

Note that the proper noun *Peter's* is the singular possessive form of *Peter* because it shows that Peter owns his shadow. It is the shadow of Peter. Later in this lesson we will return to the formation of the possessive case, the ownership case, for singular and plural nouns.

Grammar texts, standardized tests and some teachers require that we give names to the various pronouns. The list varies with names such as personal pronouns, relative pronouns, indefinite pronouns, reflexive pronouns. We will focus now only on relative pronouns and personal pronouns. Although the other names of pronouns are interesting and important, they are not as essential to the writing of sentences as the two kinds of pronouns named here.

Who versus Whom: The Mysterious "Case" of the Relative Pronoun

A relative pronoun introduces a clause that describes a noun or pronoun in the previous clause. An example can be found in the sentence *I lost the dollar that I found yesterday*. The relative pronoun *that* introduces the clause *that I found*, which describes the noun *dollar* in the previous clause. There are seven relative pronouns:

> that
> who
> whom
> which
> whose
> what
> whatever

Any clause beginning with one of these relative pronouns is called a *relative clause*. The relative clause is one kind of dependent clause.

Who and *whom* are two of these relative pronouns that deserve special attention. The mere mention of *who* or *whom* still strikes fear in the hearts of so many of us who have met these babies on standardized tests from junior high to the SAT. As I'm sure you recall, these tests ask us to choose (who, whom) usually stuck in the middle of a sentence. So let's try it now, with the following sentence:

> We are witnesses of these things, and so is the Holy Spirit, (who, whom) God has given to those (who, whom) obey him. (Acts 5:32)

I remember vividly one of my teachers giving me a fifty-question test just after school. I had fifteen minutes to get to basketball practice. I looked at the fifty pairs of (who, whom) staring back at me from the test paper; I didn't have a clue. I reached into my pocket for a quarter. Heads for *who*. Tails for *whom*. I flipped the coin fifty times because I did not know how to determine the correct answer for any one of the fifty questions. I was on time to practice; however, I learned the next day that I had missed twenty-four of the fifty questions. My quarter had failed me.

Let's figure this out so that you will never have to flip a coin as I did. Look at the verse just quoted:

> (Who, Whom) God has given to those (who, whom) obey him.

In each instance I must choose whether my answer is the subject of a verb or the object of the verb. How is this done? First, locate every verb. Then determine if each verb has a subject provided other than the subject *who*. If the verb has a subject, then my choice will be the objective form, *whom*.

The first subject-verb cluster is *God/has given*. The complete verb is *has given*; the subject is *God*. Therefore, according to our 1-2-3-step test, *whom* is the correct answer because we need the objective form. *Whom* like *him*, *them* and *us* is the objective case form of the pronoun. Look at the last clause in the verse: "(*who, whom*) obey him." If we were decorating this clause, we mark *obey* as the verb. The first priority is for the verb to have a subject. No other subject is provided; therefore, *who*, the subjective form of the pronoun, is the correct form. *Who*, incidentally, is a pronoun whose antecedent is *those* from the preceding clause.

Let's recapitulate. If we have a thousand sentences with the *who, whom* relative pronoun introducing a relative clause in the middle of the sentence, our procedure is the same. First, we locate the complete verb. If the verb has a subject provided already, the relative pronoun will take the objective case form, *whom*. If the verb has no subject provided, the subjective case form, *who*, must be the subject of the relative clause.

This *who, whom* nightmare need not trouble us anymore. I didn't have to rely on the flipping of the coin to help me choose those fifty answers. All I needed was to know to look for each verb and its subject. Every verb must have a subject. If the verb has no subject other than the *who*, then *who* is my choice. If each verb has a subject already provided, then the *whom* is the correct choice. *Whom* must be the object of the verb.

Let's look at this *who, whom* challenge one more time. The setting is Jerusalem and the authorities are upset with Peter and other apostles for having taught the people in the name of Jesus. In Acts 5 these authorities are represented by the high priest and members of the Sanhedrin, the full assembly of the elders of Israel. To the surprise of the high priest and his buddies, Peter and his friends are no longer in the public jail. Rather, they are teaching in the temple; they have been there since early morning. Acts 5:30 gives one of Peter's responses to the authorities' objections to his preaching. Again, this verse poses the *who, whom* question. I want you to choose the correct pronoun. Here's the verse:

> The God of our fathers raised Jesus from the dead—(who, whom) you had killed by hanging him on a tree. (Acts 5:30)

Again, we take our three steps. First step: locate the verb in the relative clause. The complete verb is *had killed*. Second step: locate a subject between the verb and the *who, whom* choice. The subject is *you*. When a subject is provided and if there is no verb that needs a subject, the answer has to be *whom*, the objective case form of the pronoun. In this verse both the subject and the verb are provided; therefore, the relative pronoun, *whom*, serves as the direct object of the verb. Had there been no subject provided, we have to provide one. The *who* becomes the relative pronoun subject of the verb. Look at the following sentence written by one of my students, and determine if the word *whom* is correct or incorrect. "Dr. Beaty, *whom* I thought looked like Santa Claus, was my first professor in college." What about *whom*? Explain why it is incorrect.

Nouns (Singular) in the Possessive Case

As stated earlier, nouns in English pose no problems in the subjective or objective cases because they do not change form as subjects or as objects. The following italicized nouns are singular in the possessive case. Each singular, possessive case noun is taken from a verse in Matthew's Gospel; all are from the New International Version (NIV). Read these singular possessive case nouns and look for a pattern in the italicized nouns.

Matthew 2:19b	the *child's* life
Matthew 3:4a	*John's* clothes were made of *camel's* hair
Matthew 5:34b	for it is *God's* throne
Matthew 7:5b	the speck from your *brother's* eye
Matthew 8:14	When Jesus came into *Peter's* house, he saw *Peter's* mother.

Matthew 9:9a	a man, Matthew, sitting at a tax *collector's* table
Matthew 9:10	while Jesus was having dinner at *Matthew's* house
Matthew 9:14	Then *John's* disciples came and asked him
Matthew 9:23	when Jesus entered the *ruler's* house
Matthew 10:41	a *prophet's* reward . . . a righteous *man's* reward
Matthew 11:7a	as *John's* disciples were leaving
Matthew 12:29a	how can anyone enter a strong *man's* house
Matthew 12:42b	to listen to *Solomon's* wisdom
Matthew 13:27a	the *owner's* servants came to him and said
Matthew 13:55	Isn't this the *carpenter's* son? Isn't his *mother's* name Mary?
Matthew 14:3b	because of Herodias, his brother *Philip's* wife
Matthew 14:6a	on *Herod's* birthday
Matthew 14:12a	*John's* disciples came and took his body
Matthew 16:27a	in his *Father's* glory
Matthew 18:26a	the *servant's* master
Matthew 20:20	of *Zebedee's* sons
Matthew 21:25	*John's* baptism
Matthew 22:21	what is *Caesar's* (due) and to God what is *God's* (due)
Matthew 23:1	the Pharisees sit in *Moses'* seat
Matthew 23:22	And he who swears by heaven swears by *God's* throne
Matthew 26:51	one of *Jesus'* companions reached for his sword
Matthew 27:7	to buy the *potter's* field
Matthew 27:15	now it was the *governor's* custom at the Feast
Matthew 27:9	while Pilate was sitting in the *judge's* seat
Matthew 27:24	I am innocent of this *man's* blood
Matthew 27:27	then the *governor's* soldiers
Matthew 27:56	and the mother of *Zebedee's* sons
Matthew 27:58	he asked for *Jesus'* body

Note that all but three of the italicized words end with an apostrophe (') plus the letter *s*. The *'s* is the ending of all singular possessive nouns if the word in the possessive case ends with any letter other than the letter *s*. This is precisely why forming the singular possessive case for nouns in English is so easy to write correctly. A huge percentage of singular possessive case nouns is formed by adding the apostrophe and *s* (*'s*). Say your first name; then write it in the singular possessive case.

My first name is Jim. Therefore, if I want to write about this book, I write, "Jim's book." I have a grandson named Wil. Therefore, I write, "Wil's ability to play golf astounds adult golfers." The book belongs to Jim Beaty; I write, "Jim's book." The ability to strike a golf ball belongs to Wil; therefore, I write, "Wil's ability." I have a beautiful granddaughter who has red hair. Her name is Whitner. I speak of Whitner's red hair. Wil owns the ability; Whitner owns the red hair. I own the book I have written.

I have a grandson named Jackson who lives in Orlando. I write, "Jackson's house is in Florida." Jackson's little sister is a beauty named Caroline. Caroline's big brother is Jackson. A fifteen-year-old granddaughter named McIver is Whitner's little sister. Therefore, McIver's older sister is Whitner. Trey and Beaty are two grandsons who live in Columbia, South Carolina. Trey's favorite pastime is tennis. Beaty's favorite pastime is torturing Trey. The babies of this grandchildren parade are Elijah and Jordan; they live in Virginia. Elijah's mother is named Dawn. Jordan's favorite TV personality is Stephen Colbert. Note please that the singular possessive case of the names of my grandchildren is written exactly the same way—*'s*.

The only exceptions to forming the singular possessive case occur when the singular noun has two *s* sounds. Reading the references from Matthew's Gospel, you find the names of Moses and Jesus in the possessive case. Because those two names have two *s* sounds, only the apostrophe (') is added. We do not need a third *s* sound. Matthew 23:2 reads that "the Pharisees sit in Moses' [not Moses's] seat." Matthew 26:51 reads that "one of Jesus' [not Jesus's] companions reached for his sword." Matthew 27:58 reads that "he asked for Jesus' [not Jesus's] body." Forming the singular possessive case of any noun is a piece of cake. The only tricky part is determining if the noun is to be written in the singular possessive case. Ownership requires the possessive case. *The father's glory* is correct because the glory belongs to the father. *God's throne* is correct because the throne belongs to God. *The potter's field* is correct because the field belongs to the potter. *This man's blood* is correct because the blood belongs to the man. *Wil's ability* is correct because the ability belongs to Wil. *Whitner's red hair* is correct because the red hair belongs to Whitner. Following these steps will keep us on track and will assure that we write correctly the singular possessive case of nouns. Remember, a noun names a person, a place or a thing. And the singular possessive case of nouns is as easy as ABC.

Nouns (PLURAL) in the Possessive Case

Writing the plural possessive case form of nouns is simple. But writing the correct form requires a few more steps than does the singular possessive form. Having determined that the possessive case *plural* form is needed, we take a few precise steps. Before we look at those steps, let us quote the few possessive case plurals that are in Matthew's Gospel. I am listing, for your convenience, five examples. As above, these examples come from the New International Version (NIV), and the noun in the possessive case *plural* is in **bold type**.

Matthew 11:8	No, those who wear fine clothes are in **kings'** palaces. (Two or more kings)
Matthew 15:27	Yes, Lord, she said, but even the dogs eat the crumbs that fall from their **masters'** table. (More than one master)
Matthew 23:4	They put them on **men's** shoulders
Matthew 23:13	You shut the kingdom of heaven in **men's** faces.
Matthew 23:27	Which look beautiful on the outside but on the inside are full of dead **men's** bones

Almost every time when forming the singular possessive case, we add the *'s*; child becomes *child's*. Servant becomes *servant's*. Bible becomes *Bible's*, etc.

The plural possessive adds a step or two. Step one, make sure the word has been made *plural*. Step two asks if the plural form of the noun ends with the letter *s*. If so, adding the apostrophe completes the third step in forming the plural possessive case of nouns.

Only two of the plural possessives listed from Matthew end with the letter *s*. Matthew 11:8 speaks of well-dressed folks "in kings' palaces." *Kings* is plural; we form the plural by adding the letter *s*. Adding the (') forms the correct plural possessive case form. Matthew 15:27 reads "from their masters' table." The plural form of the word *master* is *masters*, so the correct form that we find in this verse is *masters'*. Whenever the plural form of the noun ends with the letter *s*, we simply add the (') in the next space after the *s*.

Difficulty comes when the plural form of the noun does not end in *s*. Look at the other three examples from Matthew. In 23:4, the words appear *on men's shoulders*. The singular form is man. If we have two of those creatures, we have two men. Whenever the plural form of the noun does not end in *s*, we treat the plural possessive noun as though it were singular. That's why the verse correctly reads *on men's shoulders*. Matthew 23:27b reads, "Full of dead men's bones." Following these simple steps will prevent making an error in the possessive case *plural* form of a noun.

Verbs and the Cases of Pronouns

Early in our study we learned that nouns and pronouns are the only two parts of speech that have case. The case of any noun or pronoun is determined by its use in the sentence. The names of the three cases are *subjective, objective* and *possessive*. Any noun or pronoun that functions as a subject of a verb is written in the *subjective* case form. And any noun or pronoun that functions as an object in a sentence is written in the *objective* case form. Those are the nouns or pronouns that are used as direct objects of verbs, indirect objects of verbs, objects of prepositions, objects of infinitives. The third case is the *possessive* case. Any noun or pronoun that shows ownership is written in the *possessive* case form. All nouns, singular or plural, that show ownership must also show an apostrophe (').

Note the apostrophes showing in the two verses from Hebrews: "By faith **Moses'** parents hid him for three months after he was born, because they saw he was no ordinary child, and they were not afraid of the **king's** edict. By faith Moses, when he had grown up, refused to be known as the son of **Pharaoh's** daughter" (Heb. 11:23-24). The three words in **bold** type, **Moses'**, **king's** and **Pharaoh's** show the apostrophe (') because they are all singular, possessive nouns. The adding of the apostrophe (') for both the singular and the plural possessive case is the only change that occurs in nouns in the possessive case.

But pronouns behave differently from nouns in their forms for the three cases. If we consider the three forms of the pronouns *he, him* and *his*, we see three different cases: subjective (*he*), objective (*him*) and possessive (*his*). Watch how these three forms of pronouns work out in the first verse of the thirteenth chapter of John's Gospel (John 13:1):

> It was just before the Passover Feast. Jesus knew that the time had come for **him** to leave this world and go to the

Father. Having loved **his** own who were in the world, **he** now showed them the full extent of **his** love.

The four words in **bold** type, in order, are *him* (objective case), *his* (possessive case), *he* (subjective case) and *his* (possessive case). Examine all four of these pronouns in John 13:1. Determine the reason for the particular use in all four instances. The first of the four pronouns in this assertion is the word *him*. "The time had come for **him** to leave this world." The words *for him* form a two-word prepositional phrase. Early in this text we learned that a preposition is a word that joins its *object* to the rest of the sentence. The word *for* in this instance is a preposition, and the entire prepositional phrase is *for him*. Why not "for he" or "for his"? A preposition joins its *object* to the rest of the sentence; the object is written in the objective case form, and neither *he* nor *his* is the objective case form of this pronoun. They are the subjective and possessive case forms respectively.

The second pronoun in this verse is *his*, in the phrase "having loved **his** own." The possessive form of the pronoun *he* is *his*. This word *his* is the possessive pronoun form of the pronoun *he*. We are *his* own.

Examining these four pronouns enables the reader to see each pronoun's use in the verse. The first pronoun, *him* (objective case), is the object of the preposition *for*. The second pronoun, *his* (possessive case), shows ownership in the expression "loved **his** own." The third pronoun, *he* (subjective case), functions as the subject of the verb *showed*. As a subject of a verb the pronoun must be written in the subjective case form. No one who speaks English is tempted to say or write, "Him showed" or "His showed." We want to say, "*He* showed me the way."

John 20:20b reads, "**He** showed them **his** hands and **his** side."

Neither *him* nor *his* can correctly function as the subject of the verb *showed*.

Acts 1:3 reads,

> After **his** suffering, **he** showed himself to these men and gave many convincing proofs that **he** was alive. **He** appeared to them over a period of forty days and spoke about the kingdom of God.

The four pronouns in **bold** type in Acts 1:3 show us all three cases at work. Be sure you understand perfectly the case of each pronoun and be able to explain the reason for each.

Power in the Possessive Case

Let's go back to John 13:1. Even points of grammar can make our hearts sing as they apply to the written word, especially the words of the Bible. The fourth pronoun in John 13:1 is *his*, functioning as the adjective modifier of the noun *love*. Jesus possesses the love that he freely bestows upon his own. The love referred to here is his love; he possesses it. He has it and possesses it for all mankind. As some of my students enjoy saying, "That'll preach." Grammar helps us grasp powerful truths through the concept of the possessive case. Here, we can glory in the fact that those who love God do so only as they already have been loved. We love God because God first loved us.

Understanding the case of a pronoun in its context in the sentence makes for correctness. If a pronoun is the subject of a verb, the pronoun must be written in the subjective case form. If the pronoun is a grammatical object, the pronoun must be written in the objective case form. If the pronoun shows possession or ownership, the pronoun must be written in the possessive case form.

Self-Quiz for Chapter Two: The Case for the Three Cases

1. Name the three cases in English.
2. What two parts of speech have case?
3. How many of the remaining six parts of speech have case?
4. A noun or pronoun following a preposition (in a prepositional phrase) is written in what case?
5. The part of a sentence before (in front of) a verb is called what "territory"?
6. The part of a sentence following (after) a verb is called what "territory"?
7. The pronouns *I, he, she, they, we* and *who* are always what case?
8. The pronouns *me, them, us* and *whom* are always what case?
9. The pronouns *his, hers, our, their* and *whose* are always what case?

10. List seven relative pronouns.
11. What do relative pronouns introduce?
12. What do relative pronouns do to the clause that follows them?
13. Why is the singular possessive case of Jesus and Moses written with the apostrophe (') immediately following the second *s*?
14. What is the case of a noun or pronoun that follows a preposition in the prepositional phrase?

Exercises for Chapter Two: The Case for the Three Cases

1. Write ten pronouns.
2. Be sure that these pronouns are on 3 × 5 cards for your reviewing.
3. Write seven relative pronouns.
4. Write five sentences that have relative pronouns that introduce relative, subordinate clauses.
5. Name the three cases that nouns and pronouns can have in sentences.

THREE

The Simple Sentence

First Things First: The Clause

What's the big deal about the clause? The clause is the basic building block of the sentence. It is the heart of the sentence; without a clause there can be no sentence. But more simply put, a clause is a group of related words that contains a subject and a verb.

Learn this definition right now. Say it aloud: "A clause is a group of related words that contains a subject and a verb." Write it two times in your special *Sacred Grammar* notebook, separate from your textbook. Make flash cards using 3 × 5 index cards. Write the word *clause* on the unlined side of the card, and on the lined side of the card write, "A clause is a group of related words that contains a subject and a verb."

Learn the Correct Definition of the Predicate

Some teachers and most grammar books use the word *predicate* interchangeably with the word *verb*. That is all right to do, except that few of us know the definition of a predicate. In order to clear the air, let's say for now that a predicate is the verb and the words that follow the verb to the end of the clause. For example, Isaiah 62:6a reads, "I have posted watchmen on your walls." The complete verb in this sentence is *have posted* while the predicate is *have posted watchmen on your walls*. I would make another flash card with the word *predicate* written on the unlined side of the card and the definition written on the lined side of the card. The predicate is the verb in addition to the word or words that follow it to the end of its clause. Repeat this definition until you know it cold.

You have learned that a clause is a group of related words that contains a subject and a verb. The only two kinds of clauses are independent and dependent. The independent clause does not have a changing word in front of what is called the subject-verb cluster. The only two groups of changing words, or subordinators, are subordinate conjunctions and relative pronouns. John 11:35, the shortest verse in the Bible, is an independent clause. That verse reads, "Jesus wept." The successful editing of sentences depends upon the ability to recognize the independent clause. If I write a dependent clause and I think I have written an independent clause, I have erred because I have, in fact, written a fragment. A fragment is never a sentence. Fragments are to be avoided, especially if I have tricked myself into thinking I have written a sentence. Some fragments are allowable, even helpful, when intentional. Certainly, I can write, "Glory to God!" or "Oh, what a day!" But I want to be sure that I know that I have not written a sentence. Fragments in writing remind me of bases on balls or walks in baseball. The intentional base on balls is a good thing when putting a batter on base enables making an out or two with the next batter. Intentional fragments work. Unintentional fragments blemish otherwise good writing.

I love to ask my students if the expression "Jesus wept" is a sentence. When I pose the question to secular university students, they say that it is not a sentence. I ask them why is "Jesus wept" not a sentence. They say that it's too short. I ask my Bible College students if the expression "Jesus wept" is a sentence. Without hesitation, they answer that it is a sentence. I ask why. They say because it's in the Bible. Obviously, neither group understands; both have given wrong reasons for their answers. "Jesus wept" is a sentence because it is an independent clause.

The number of words has nothing to do with determining whether a group of words forms a sentence. The presence of an independent clause is all you need to make a sentence. And the simple sentence has only one independent clause. The simple sentence may have two subjects and two verbs and modifiers and phrases. But the simple sentence has only one independent clause. In the five following examples of independent clauses (simple sentences) from the Hebrew Bible and from New Testament verses, you can see the great variety that is possible in the simple sentence.

Jeremiah 5:11 reads, "The house of Israel and the house of Judah have been utterly unfaithful to me." Let's take a walk through and investigate why this is a simple sentence with various decorations. In editing sentences we first find the verb that shows action or state of being. Then we find the subject of the verb. That is the word or words that identify the action taking place or the state of being that is occurring. The verb here is a state of being verb. The two words *have been* are the complete verb, showing a state of being. We might be tempted to call *unfaithful* the verb. That cannot be because *unfaithful* is not a verb; it is an adjective. If you are ever unsure whether a word is a verb, go straight to the word in your dictionary.

Jeremiah 5:11 contains one state of being verb. The two subjects are the two nouns *house* and *house*. Note that each of the two words, *house*, has a prepositional phrase following it: *house of Israel* and *house of Judah*. I want you to determine why neither Israel nor Judah can be the subject of the verb. You are right! They are objects of the prepositions, and a word cannot function as two different cases at the same moment. Remember Churchill's playing with the preposition. The prepositional phrase is our friend in that, besides offering us helpful or descriptive information, it helps us locate the subject of the verb. We have two subjects, the words *house*, joined by the coordinate conjunction *and*. This is a compound subject, but the sentence contains only one independent clause. The two subjects (compound subject) have only one verb, *have been*. Therefore, the sentence is a simple sentence. Get into the habit of locating the complete verb, then its subject and then check to see if there is a word in front of the subject-verb cluster that is either a subordinate conjunction or a relative pronoun. If no subordinator is present in front of the subject-verb cluster, the clause is independent. Thus, our one independent clause in Jeremiah 5:11 forms a simple sentence. We will look later more extensively at sentence patterns, but for now, we can note everything that this sentence contains. In addition to the compound subject and verb, it contains two prepositional phrases *of Israel* and *of Judah* in the subjective territory and the prepositional phrase *to me* in the objective territory. This meticulous scrutiny is what we want to learn to apply to all sentences that we write. It might seem awkward at first, but the process will become easier, even automatic, the more you practice.

Let's look now at another type of simple sentence from the Hebrew Bible. Amos 5:11a reads, "You trample on the poor and force him to give you grain." While Jeremiah 5:11 contains two subjects, Amos 5:11a contains two active verbs, *trample* and *force*. The subject of this compound verb is clearly *you*. No changing word appears in front of the subject-verb cluster. The only clause is independent; therefore, we have a simple sentence with two verbs, called a compound verb. These two simple sentences show us examples of both a compound subject and a compound verb. Both sentences are simple sentences because each contains only one independent clause. The last four words of this sentence, *to give you grain*, form an infinitive phrase that we need not discuss now. Our upcoming lesson on verbals will address infinitives and infinitive phrases.

The third simple sentence comes from the pen of St. Paul in his letter to the church at Ephesus. Ephesians 1:4a reads, "For he chose us in him before the creation of the world to be holy and blameless in his sight." This is a simple sentence. It contains one independent clause, *he chose*. The only word in front of the subject-verb cluster is *for*. Is *for* a changing word, either a subordinate conjunction or a relative pronoun? No, it is not. What part of speech is *for*? If you answer coordinate conjunction, you are correct. Coordinate conjunctions do not subordinate clauses. Only subordinate conjunctions and relative pronouns as changing words make clauses dependent. *For he chose* is an independent clause and could be a correct sentence if Paul had chosen to end the sentence with the word *chose*.

I have chosen Ephesians 1:4a as an example of the simple sentence for two reasons. One, coordinate conjunctions do not subordinate clauses. Most grammar texts ask us to remember coordinate conjunctions with the acronym FANBOYS. These seven letters stand for *for*, *and*, *nor*, *but*, *or*, *yet* and *so*. Memorize these seven coordinate conjunctions. My second reason for using Ephesians 1:4a is to show that the sentence begins with *for*, a coordinate conjunction. I encourage my students to begin sentences sparingly with coordinate conjunctions, especially *and* and *but*. Without exception, every time that I encourage my classes to begin sentences with coordinate conjunctions, a student tells me that she was taught never to begin a sentence with an *and* or a *but*. Other students join the chorus, citing English teachers and sometimes college professors. I answer my students that they must follow the instructions of their teachers when writing in their classes. However, I delight in citing E. B. White, perhaps America's leading essayist; Harold Bloom, a genius of indomitable brilliance; and Martin Luther King, Jr., arguably the greatest orator of the twentieth century. These three worthies begin sentences, sparingly, with coordinate conjunctions. Sentences that begin with coordinate conjunctions appear in E. B. White's essays, Bloom's *Shakespeare* (284) and King's Washington Monument speech. Please don't let me get you into trouble with your teachers or your editors. Write for them as they wish. But keep in mind that if they say "no" to *and* and *but* at the beginning of sentences, they are disagreeing with the majority of accomplished writers, including the writer of the book of Revelation:

> And God will wipe away every tear from their eyes. (Rev. 7:17)

The Bible practically *begins* with "*And God said*" six times in the first chapter of Genesis alone: Gen. 1:3, 1:6, 1:9, 1:14, 1:20, 1:24.

Following the independent clause in Ephesians 1:4a, the sentence contains a direct object, *us*. Then the great writer strings together five phrases, four prepositional phrases with one infinitive phrase placed among them. Again, we will look at the infinitive phrase when we get to the lesson on verbals.

In the fourth Gospel, John 4:43 provides a teachable sentence: "After the two days he left for Galilee." Following our same steps for editing, we see that the action verb is *left*. Its pronoun subject is *he*. So the subject-verb cluster is *he left*. Our next step is to determine if there is a changing word directly in front of the subject-verb cluster. There is not. But notice the first word in the sentence. It is *after*. This can confuse even the enlightened because the word *after* can be either a subordinate conjunction or a preposition. Here, it is a preposition because its object is *days*. *After* in this sentence begins the prepositional phrase *after the two days*. This prepositional phrase does not subordinate the independent clause that follows. This sentence from John's Gospel contains only one independent clause. It is a simple sentence. I say this verse is "teachable" because it shows that the word *after* functions as a preposition. *After* is a subordinate conjunction only if it subordinates a clause that immediately follows it. Clearly, this clause is independent; one independent clause makes a simple sentence. The last two words of this simple sentence are *for Galilee*, our old friend the prepositional phrase. Your lists of subordinate conjunctions and prepositions should include both the words *after* and *for*. You know now that *after* is a preposition when it starts a phrase, and *after* is a subordinate conjunction when it introduces a dependent clause. The same is true for the word *for*.

Our fifth simple sentence comes from Acts 20:24a: "However, I consider my life worth nothing to me." The action verb is *consider* with the pronoun subject *I*. Checking for a subordinator reveals there is none because the only word in front of the subject-verb cluster is *however*. This useful word, *however*, is a conjunctive adverb. The only changing words that make a clause dependent are subordinate conjunctions and relative pronouns. Conjunctive adverbs do not subordinate clauses. This heart-rending sentence from Paul is a simple sentence because no changing word appears directly in front of the subject-verb cluster and because there is only one clause in the sentence.

Valuable information is ours from this review of simple sentences. Every simple sentence by definition contains only one independent clause. Additionally, we see that this first of the four kinds of sentences has virtually unlimited variations. It often has two subjects or two verbs with phrases and modifiers. From the simple sentence we will now build the remaining three: the complex sentence, the compound sentence and the compound-complex sentence.

But first let's check to see where we are in our learning journey. Master the little quiz and the writing exercises for this lesson.

Self-Quiz for Chapter Three: The Simple Sentence

1. Define a clause.
2. Name the two kinds of clauses.
3. In our system what is a changing word?
4. The two groups of changing words are called what?
5. What is the shortest verse in the Bible? What does it say?
6. What is a fragment?
7. How is an intentionally written fragment like an intentional walk or base on balls in baseball?
8. Why is "Jesus wept" a sentence?
9. Why is "Then Jesus wept" a sentence?
10. Why is "When Jesus wept" a fragment?
11. What is the one requirement in order to have a sentence?
12. What kind of clause does a simple sentence never have?
13. Can a simple sentence have two subjects and two verbs?
14. In Jeremiah 5:11 what part of speech is the word *unfaithful*?
15. Every verb denotes either _____ or _____.
16. Are the two verbs in Amos 5:11a action or state of being verbs?
17. What is the importance of the acronym FANBOYS?
18. Write seven coordinate conjunctions.
19. When is the word *after* a preposition?
20. When is the word *after* a subordinate conjunction?

21. What do E. B. White, Harold Bloom and Martin Luther King, Jr., have in common?
22. The word *however* is a conjunctive adverb. Does it make a clause that follows it dependent?
23. List ten conjunctive adverbs.
24. List ten subordinate conjunctions.
25. Who won the 2010 World Series?

Writing Exercises for Chapter Three: The Simple Sentence

1. Write on separate paper all five of the verses from the Bible that we examined in this lesson. Underline with two lines each complete verb; underline with one line each subject, and place (parentheses) around each phrase.
2. Write five simple sentences. Underline verbs and subjects exactly as you did in the five verses. Then place (parentheses) around all the phrases that you have written.

FOUR

The Complex Sentence

    We have learned that the simple sentence contains only one independent clause, and one independent clause is a simple sentence. We have learned that subordination changes an independent clause to a dependent clause. The only two groups of changing words are subordinate conjunctions (*although*, *because*, *even though*, etc.) and relative pronouns (*that*, *who*, *whom*, *which*, etc.). The complex sentence contains only one independent clause and one or more dependent clauses. We have said that the prepositional phrase is a friend of the writer because by recognizing it, we more easily determine subject-verb agreement. The complex sentence is another friend of the writer. Dependent clauses help sentences flow within paragraphs the way water flows over rocks in a mountain stream. Too many simple sentences strung back to back, on the other hand, make for very dull reading. Imagine paragraphs with nothing but simple sentences. How horrible. For instance, "He hit the ball. The ball cleared the fence. The fence is six feet tall." We certainly want to use the simple sentence. However, no accomplished writer wants to write the same of anything over and over. Understanding how to form complex sentences is one way to assure variety in our writing and especially in the way we begin sentences.

    What if the passage in Judges 8:27 were written as a series of simple sentences? Gideon made the gold into an ephod. He placed the ephod in Ophrah. Ophrah was his town. All Israel prostituted themselves. They worshipped it there. It became a snare to Gideon. It became a snare to his family.

    Now, here it is using a variety of phrases and clauses: "Gideon made the gold into an ephod, which he placed in Ophrah, his town. All Israel prostituted themselves by worshipping it there, and it became a snare to Gideon and his family."

Think of the complex sentence as a continuation of the simple sentence. The simple sentence contains only one independent clause. The complex sentence is only one independent clause in addition to at least one dependent clause. Look again at John 11:35, "Jesus wept." That independent clause becomes a dependent clause when a subordinator is placed in front of it. The subordinator is the changing word that makes the clause dependent. As stated already, the two types of subordinators are subordinate conjunctions and relative pronouns. I have waited until now, in this complex sentence lesson, to write a full list of subordinate conjunctions and relative pronouns. Be sure to memorize these two groups thoroughly.

Subordinate conjunctions: after, although, as, as if, as soon as, as though, because, before, even if, even though, how, if, in case, in that, insofar as, no matter how, now that, once, provided that, since, so that, than, though, unless, until, when, whenever, where, wherever, whether, while.

Relative pronouns: that, who, whom, which, whose, what, whatever.

Note that a word is a subordinator only when it appears in front of a subject-verb cluster. A few subordinate conjunctions such as *after* and *before* perform also as prepositions when no subject-verb cluster follows. Whenever they are prepositions, they introduce or begin the prepositional phrase that follows. The preposition is the word that joins its object, always a noun or pronoun, to the rest of the sentence. Let's take a moment to look at some examples from the Bible of *after* and *before* being used as prepositions:

> These wicked people go after other gods to serve and worship them. (Jer. 13:10)

The words *after other gods* form a prepositional phrase; *after* is the preposition that joins its object, *gods*, to the rest of the sentence. Note that there is no subject-verb cluster following *after* in this sentence.

> And he says in another place, thou art a priest forever after the order of Melchizedek. (Heb. 5:6 KJV)

Again, *after* is a preposition that joins its noun object, *order*, to the rest of the sentence. The word *after* in both these verses is a preposition that joins or connects its object to the rest of the sentence. A large percentage of all the words we write will form prepositional phrases. Perhaps they occur so frequently because they add so much extra information to our sentences.

Neither *after* in either example above can be called a subordinate conjunction as neither created a dependent clause. Get into the habit of determining how words function in segments. The two main segments of all sentences are clauses and phrases. Phrases, many kinds, live inside clauses. Distinguishing the difference between the two will make editing sentences a pleasant chore.

Before is another word that can function either as a subordinate conjunction or as a preposition. Study the two *before* phrases that follow:

> And all the six hundred Gittites who had accompanied him
> from Gath marched before the king. (2 Sam. 15:18b)

Before the king is a prepositional phrase. The word *king* is the noun object of the preposition *before* and is joined to the rest of the sentence in this cozy little phrase. In your study of the scriptures, you will note dozens of examples showing how words can function as two or more parts of speech. These three Bible references suffice for now. For this lesson on the complex sentence, we need only to remember that a subordinate conjunction or relative pronoun becomes a subordinator when it precedes a subject-verb cluster, thereby building a dependent clause.

Let us go now to the friendly area of the complex sentence. Earlier we looked into Matthew's Gospel for singular and plural nouns written in the possessive case. Space will not permit our reviewing all the complex sentences Mark penned. However, we will look at a sampling in order to show how this earliest of the four Gospels is full of complex sentences. We don't have to read far in any good writing to discover the complex sentence.

Mark 1:10 contains the first complex sentence of the second Gospel. All four Gospels were written originally in Greek, and obviously, all are translated into English. The structure of Greek sentences and English sentences, however, is similar. Mark 1:10 is a complex sentence in both Greek and English. Look at the NIV translation of this verse that describes Jesus' baptism:

> As Jesus was coming up out of the water, he saw heaven being torn open and the Spirit descending on him like a dove.

We define the complex sentence as one that contains only one independent clause and at least one dependent clause. We search for each clause first by locating the subject-verb cluster. The action indicated in the first clause from Mark 1:10 comes to the reader in two words: *was coming*. The actor or the one performing the action is the subject, *Jesus*. The subject-verb cluster, *Jesus was coming*, builds the clause.

Next, we run the clause test that tells us whether the clause is independent or dependent.

If no changing word appears immediately in front of the subject of the verb, the clause is independent. If a changing word does appear in front of the subject-verb cluster, the clause is dependent. In this beginning clause in Mark 1:10, the word *as* changes an otherwise independent clause to a dependent clause. Lists in grammar texts always include some form of the subordinate conjunction, *as*. So the first clause of the sentence telling us of Jesus' baptism is clearly dependent; it is subordinated by the changing word *as*. Most readers would say that "As Jesus came up out of the water" is not a complete sentence. What do you say? The readers are correct. The evidence that this is a dependent clause rests in the presence of the subordinate conjunction *as*. Because this clause begins with *as,* it cannot stand alone as a sentence. If we tried to let it stand alone, it would simply remain a fragment, which is a basic writing error. For this reason we consider such a clause dependent. In writing, a dependent clause offers only a partial thought or message. It needs an independent clause to form a complete thought.

Note that grammar texts and grammar teachers use various terms for the dependent clause. Other names for the dependent clause include introductory clause, subordinate clause and adverbial clause. Don't be confused by the different terms. Simply understand what each one means. The name introductory clause is not used simply because the clause comes first in the sentence. The name implies correctly that this clause exists to introduce and is therefore dependent upon an independent clause that will follow. The word subordinate means that the clause is subordinate to, or ranked beneath, the independent clause. The indication mechanism for this subordinate clause is the actual presence of one of the changing words. The two groups of changing words are subordinate conjunctions (*as*, *whether*, etc.) and relative pronouns (*that*, *who*, *what*, etc.). See above the more comprehensive lists of subordinate conjunctions and relative pronouns.

Another type of dependent clause, the adverbial clause, functions as an adverb, usually modifying the verb in the clause that follows. In Mark 1:10, the clause "As Jesus was coming up out of the water" is dependent. It is introductory, it is subordinate, it is adverbial. In this text, *Sacred Grammar*, the term *dependent clause* is the one I have chosen to use most. Think of clauses as either independent or dependent. Independent clauses have no changing words in front of the subject-verb cluster. Dependent clauses must have a changing word subordinator in front of the subject. Changing words provide the evidence necessary to prove a clause is dependent. The dependent clause written alone is a fragment and cannot stand as a sentence. The unintentional fragment is an error, as well as an independent thought or message, and it should be avoided.

The second clause in Mark 1:10 proves to be independent; its subject-verb cluster reads *he saw*. No hint of a subordinator is present to indicate that the clause is dependent. So far in Mark 1:10, we have a dependent clause followed by the independent clause *he saw*. Read the rest of the sentence. Do you see any more verbs? Be careful; finding this answer can be difficult. The word *heaven* is the direct object because it answers the question, what receives the action of the verb? The remaining words, which complete the predicate, are "being torn open and the Spirit descending on him like a dove." If you, like so many, are tempted to name *being* and *descending* as verbs, don't do it. These *ing* words look and sound like verbs; they are not. *Descending* certainly implies the action of falling. However, neither *being* nor *descending* in this sentence is a verb. Indeed, the words do come from verb stems *to be* and *to descend*. These stem forms (to) are called infinitives: *to act, to be, to call, to evangelize, to fall, to love*. But these verblike words, like *being* and *descending* in this case, without helping verbs to complete them, are called *verbals*; they are not verbs.

Whenever you are tempted to name an *ing* word a verb, run this little test. Just say your first name in front of an *ing* verbal or in front of an infinitive. I'll do it with you. Jim acting. Jim being. Jim calling. Jim loving. Not one of these pairs of words forms a subject-verb cluster. Not one meets the definition of a clause. Not one is a group of words that contains a subject and a verb. Try the same exercise with infinitives: Jim to act. Jim to be. Jim to call. Jim to write. Again, not one of these attempts forms a sentence. Each is a fragment and cannot parade as a sentence.

I want you to understand that Mark 1:10 is a complex sentence that begins with a dependent clause followed by the independent clause *he saw*. Remember that John 11:35, "Jesus wept," is a sentence because it is an independent clause. The remainder of the sentence in Mark 1:10 after the verb meets our definition of a predicate. As we stated, *heaven* is the direct object of the verb. It is followed by two verbal phrases introduced by the words *being* and *descending*. We need not bother with these verbals now. That lesson comes later. For now, we note that the words of Mark's complex sentence fit perfectly. Detailed scrutiny of every word in this complex sentence (Mark 1:10) gives an example of one of many patterns that we can learn and make our own in our writing.

Read Mark 1:14. "After John was put in prison, Jesus went into Galilee, proclaiming the good news of God."

Note the similar pattern to Mark 1:10. The first clause is dependent and is made dependent by the subordinate conjunction *after*. You will recall that three questions comprise our clause test. One, is there a verb? Two, does the verb have a subject? Three, is there a changing word right in front of the subject? Three yeses indicate that the clause is dependent. The second clause in the sentence is "Jesus went into Galilee, proclaiming the good news of God." Again, begin with the search for the verb, the word or words that show action or state of being. The verb in this second clause is *went*. The one doing the action is the subject, *Jesus*. This subject-verb cluster has no changing word, no subordinate conjunction or relative pronoun preceding it. Therefore, this *Jesus went* clause is independent. The six words following the word *Galilee* complete the predicate. Note the word *proclaiming*. Again, it looks and sounds like a verb. It is what I like to call verbish. But it is not a verb. It is one of the three verbals that we will master in a later lesson.

The words proclaiming the good news form a verbal phrase, in this case, a participial phrase. In chapter 9, we will learn the three verbals: gerunds, participles and infinitives. Our task in this chapter is to understand that these two verses, Mark 1:10 and Mark 1:14, are both complex sentences. Both begin with dependent clauses, made dependent by changing words called subordinate conjunctions, *as* and *after*. Both have independent clauses following the opening dependent clauses. Both sentences conclude with verbal phrases that do not qualify as clauses. These sentences reveal patterns used often by accomplished writers. Make them part of your sentence arsenal. Make yourself thoroughly familiar with every segment of these sentences. Be able to explain to yourself how each part of the sentence fits with every other part.

Let's review a bit. Understand that the first group of related words in Mark 1:10 and in Mark 1:14 is a dependent clause. The change-making words in front of the subject-verb clusters respectively are the subordinate conjunctions *as* and *after*. The next group of related words forms an independent clause followed by phrases built on verbals. The complex sentence contains only one independent clause and one or more dependent clauses. Therefore, both of these sentences that we have enjoyed are complex by definition.

Let me say it yet again. All complex sentences have only one independent clause in addition to one or more dependent clauses. But complex sentences can vary in the relative positions of their different clauses. Mark's Gospel features many kinds of complex sentences. And they are excellent examples for us to follow in our writing.

Another verse, still in the first chapter of Mark, throws good light on the study of the complex sentence. Mark 1:22 is a nugget that reveals what the people thought of Jesus as a teacher. These people, yearning and hungry to be taught, found a diamond in the rough. At the same time this verse teaches a model of the complex sentence. The New International Version of verse twenty-two reads, "The people were amazed at his teaching because he taught them as one who had authority, not as a teacher of the law."

The content of this verse brings Jesus into high definition. He shines while teachers of the law pale into gloomy insignificance. The verse bristles with power. "The people were amazed at his teaching because he taught them as one who had authority, not as teachers of the law." Mark 1:22 provides a classic complex sentence. The first seven words contain a subject-verb cluster with no changing word. If these seven words were all we had in the sentence, the independent clause would make it a simple sentence and a complete thought in itself. But two dependent clauses follow. One is introduced with the subordinate conjunction *because*. The *who had authority* clause is made dependent by the relative pronoun *who*, which is also the subject of the verb *had*. Remember the opening clause is not introductory unless it has been made dependent with a changing-word subordinator. This complex sentence features three clauses, two dependent clauses following an independent clause. Later in this text we will delight ourselves with the study of the comma. But notice that this sentence contains not a single comma. Comma rules will come later; no comma is called for in this sentence.

By now you want to have established the habit of applying the clause test each time you write a sentence. Only three steps occur. Locate the verb. Find its subject. Search for a changing-word subordinator in front of the subject-verb cluster. If no subordinator is present, the clause is independent, and already a sentence is born. The clearest definition of a sentence is a group of words that contains at least one independent clause. It certainly may have additional clauses as does Mark 1:22. But where no independent clause appears, there is no hope of a sentence.

Mark 1:22 opens with the independent clause that reflects the people's assessment of Jesus' teaching. The phrase that closes the sentence juxtaposes Jesus with the teachers of the law. Sandwiched between the independent clause and the closing phrase are two dependent clauses and a tiny prepositional phrase *as one*. Held to the definition of the complex sentence, this one measures up. It contains only one independent clause and one or more dependent clauses.

One of the basic requirements of understanding subordination is the familiarity with words that are subordinate conjunctions and relative pronouns. I ask my students to learn at least a dozen subordinate conjunctions. Also, I ask that they memorize a few subordinate conjunctions that consist of more than one word. For instance, *as soon as, as though* and *even though* are several that should be learned.

Look at Mark 1:29: "As soon as they left the synagogue, they went with James and John to the home of Simon and Andrew."

As soon as is a subordinate conjunction. It is a changing word that subordinates or renders dependent any clause that follows it. Mark wrote it that way. I recommend that we do the same.

Let me say a word about sentence patterns. I do not recommend that we memorize certain sentence patterns. I do ask that we be able to identify the different patterns of various kinds of sentences. By the time we finish this text, I hope that the reader will be able to edit any sentence in it or any sentence the student might compose. When I edit my own sentences, the sentences I am composing just now for example, I apply the clause test we have discussed. I "decorate" each sentence. We will have a lesson later on decoration. If I have a bumpy sentence where the parts don't mesh readily, I throw out my sentence and start over. And this happens more than I want you to know. I revise; I revise, and I revise again. But I revise only after I have set down the clauses and phrases in what I feel to be a harmonious flow.

Grammar is all about editing. Editing is all about clarity. I require that my students succeed in grammar tests. But passing grammar tests is only the first step out of the blocks. For most people learning grammar is a boring, fruitless exercise unless they can apply to their writing what they have gained. Many hurdles must be cleared before we finish the race.

There's more to be said about the three complex sentences in Mark 1:10, Mark 1:14 and Mark 1:22. The patterns of the first two are almost identical. They both begin with dependent (introductory) clauses subordinated by subordinate conjunctions. Both those dependent clauses are followed by independent clauses, which have various phrases trailing them. I want you to see several gems gathered here. Please notice in these sentences and in all the sentences that you will write how each sentence begins. In editing we want to determine precisely how each sentence begins, what specific words we use. Mark, the writer, begins Mark 1:10 and Mark 1:22 with two different subordinate conjunctions. The independent clauses that follow in each of these two verses qualify these groups of words to be sentences. One independent clause all by itself makes a simple sentence. Adding more clauses changes the simple sentence to one of the other three kinds of sentences. They are complex, compound and compound-complex. In each of these two verses, we experience only one independent and only one dependent clause.

You should have a 3 × 5 index card that reads "complex sentence" on the unlined side. The lined side of the card should read, "A complex sentence is a group of related words that contains only one independent clause and one or more dependent clauses." For good measure I would write out these model sentences that we are citing from the Gospels. Their grammar as well as their content is valuable.

The benefit of using these 3 × 5 cards as flash cards is its remarkable effectiveness. I have students who have made the flash cards, then promptly placed them in a desk drawer or a pocketbook, never to look at them again. The procedure then becomes a waste of time, paper and intelligence. On the other hand I have had students who diligently plowed through their stack of flash cards faithfully in three or four sittings a week. The latter group mastered subordinate conjunctions, relative pronouns, coordinate conjunctions, conjunctive adverbs, prepositions, the parts of speech chart, the three cases, the four kinds of sentences and four comma rules, just to name a few! I hope that you will give yourself the satisfaction of learning quickly and easily by categorizing clearly the different segments of the English sentence.

You want your sentence arsenal loaded with the variations of the complex sentence.

Mark 1:35 offers yet another version of the complex sentence. The first and third clauses are dependent with the independent clause sandwiched between them. Mark 1:35 reads, "Very early (adverbial phrase) in the morning (prepositional phrase) while it was still dark, Jesus got up, left the house and went off to a solitary place, where he prayed."

The two short phrases at the beginning of this sentence both modify the three verbs in the independent clause that tells what Jesus did. But the first clause, *while it was still dark*, is dependent. The verb is *was* and its subject is *it*. The changing word is *while*. Therefore this five-word clause, with *while* as the subordinate conjunction, is dependent. The next independent clause has Jesus doing three things before daybreak. He *got* up and *left* and *went*. That's three verbs and one subject. If the words "Jesus got up, left the house and went off to a solitary place" were the whole of this verse, the sentence would be simple. But this group of words is not alone. Rather it is flanked by a clause in front of it and one behind it. The dependent clause is the group of three words, *where he prayed*. The verb is *prayed*, the subject is *he*, the changing-word subordinator is the subordinate conjunction *where*.

We learn several important grammatical points from this sentence. First, the independent clause contains a compound verb. Compound means more than one, in this case three verbs. The next point to note is that complex sentences have no boundaries as far as arrangement of clauses and phrases is concerned. Note the arrangement. We have two tiny phrases, a short dependent clause, an independent clause with three verbs and another short dependent clause. This variety liberates and inspires us to do the very same thing in our writing. So far we have chosen four verses from the Gospel of Mark, and we are not yet out of the first chapter. This frequent use of the complex sentence is not just good writing; it's the Bible.

I want us to understand that the complex sentence permeates the Gospel of Mark. The sentences vary in the placement of the subordinators. The dependent clauses are located at the beginning, middle and end of the sentences. Within the complex sentence there can be one or several dependent clauses. Those clauses can be made dependent by the two changing-word groups, subordinate conjunctions or relative pronouns. Earlier the Parts of Speech Chart emphasized that prepositions and conjunctions form the Connector Tunnel. While prepositions join their noun or pronoun objects to the rest of the sentence, subordinate conjunctions join their dependent clauses to the rest of the sentence. The relative pronoun is the other changing word whose presence makes the clause dependent. I have marked every complex sentence in both Mark and Luke. Complex sentences are everywhere, and they are there for our spiritual and syntactical improvement.

Randomly, I go to the tenth chapter of Mark's Gospel. I want you to examine the following verses to determine why each is a complex sentence. If the complex sentence is clear as you read each verse, you are ready to move on to chapter 5, "The Compound Sentence." If you do not see any of the following sentences to be complex, review this chapter for clarification.

> Therefore what God has joined together, let man not separate. (Mark 10:9)

What four words form the independent clause? The correct answer is *let man not separate*. What relative pronoun is the changing word that subordinates the dependent clause in this verse? The changing word is the relative pronoun *what*. Understand please that *therefore* is a conjunctive adverb and is not a changing-word subordinator.

> When they were in the house again, the disciples asked Jesus about this. (Mark 10:10)

What is the dependent clause in Mark 10:10? It is *When they were in the house again*. What changing word makes the clause dependent? The changing word is the subordinate conjunction *when*. Is *about this* a clause or a phrase? The words *about this* form a phrase, a group of related words that do not contain a subject-verb cluster.

> And if she divorces her husband and marries another man, she commits adultery. (Mark 10:12)

What three words form the independent clause? What word subordinates the dependent clause? What is its part of speech? This sentence begins with the dreaded *and*. Is it correct? Does *and* ever subordinate a clause? The word *and* is a coordinate conjunction and never subordinates a clause.

> When Jesus saw this he was indignant. (Mark 10:14)

What is the independent clause? The independent clause is *he was indignant*. What is the dependent clause? The dependent clause is *When Jesus saw this*. What word makes the clause dependent? The subordinate conjunction *when* makes the clause dependent. Notice that there is no comma after the word *this*. Later in our chapter on commas, we will learn the following comma rule: place a comma after long introductory clauses and phrases. Long is six or more words. This introductory clause, *When Jesus saw this*, contains only four words; therefore, no comma is needed.

> As Jesus started on his way, a man ran up to him and fell on his knees before him. (Mark 10:17)

Note the thirteen words that form the independent clause. Note the changing word *as* that makes the other clause dependent. This is a complex sentence with one independent clause and one dependent clause. Note please that two verbs such as *ran* and *fell* in Mark 10:17 form what is called a compound verb. Two verbs make a compound verb. Two independent clauses make a compound sentence.

> He went away sad because he had great wealth. (Mark 10:22b)

What is the independent clause? The independent clause is *He went away sad*. What is the changing word in the dependent clause? The changing word is the subordinate conjunction *because*. No comma appears between the clauses. What part of speech is *sad* and what word does it modify (describe)? The word *sad* describes the pronoun *he*; therefore, *sad* is an adjective. As we learned in chapter one, adjectives modify or describe only nouns and pronouns.

> You don't know what you are asking. (Mark 10:38a)

What is the subordinate clause? The subordinate clause is *what you are asking*. What is the changing-word subordinator that forms the dependent clause? The changing word is the relative pronoun *what*. There is no comma rule, by the way, that asks for a comma anywhere in this sentence.

> When the ten heard about this, they became indignant with James and John. (Mark 10:41)

What is the independent clause? The independent clause is *they became indignant with James and John.* What is the dependent (introductory) clause? The dependent, introductory clause is *When the ten heard about this.* What is the changing-word subordinate conjunction that makes the clause dependent? The subordinate conjunction that makes the clause dependent is *when.*

All these verses from the pen of Mark show the vast variety and shades of the complex sentence. They, along with dozens more, are at our disposal. On your own you now have the knowledge to locate complex sentences in and out of the Bible. Why do I ask that you examine these verses from the Bible? I have three reasons. One, I want you to recognize complex sentences and incorporate them into your writing. Two, I want you to see firsthand that the writers of the Bible mastered the complex sentence and gave us models to follow. Three, examining sentences in Holy Scripture for grammatical enlightenment will yield spiritual enlightenment as well. Besides, it's fun.

Self-Quiz Chapter Four: The Complex Sentence

1. Define the simple sentence.
2. Define the complex sentence.
3. Define subordination.
4. What is meant in this lesson by changing word?
5. What is the first complex sentence in the Gospel of Mark?
6. Name the two categories of words that are the changing words.
7. The New Testament was written originally in what language?
8. What is a subject-verb cluster and what does it form?
9. What is a sentence fragment?
10. List ten subordinate conjunctions. Be sure to include three that have in them two or more words.
11. List seven relative pronouns.
12. List two coordinate conjunctions that may be used to begin sentences.
13. How do complex sentences create a "flow" within paragraphs?
14. What two groups of words give evidence of subordination?
15. What are three additional names for the dependent clause?
16. What is the name of words that come from verbs, look like verbs and have every indication of being verbs but are not verbs?

17. In order to determine if a clause is independent or independent, we ask what three questions for our clause test?
18. Name the three cases in English.
19. Explain the three steps necessary to form the plural possessive case form of nouns.
20. Name the talented and brilliant manager of the Atlanta Braves Baseball Club who retired following the 2010 season?

FIVE

The Compound Sentence

Two or more independent clauses form the compound sentence. We have mentioned subordination that changes the independent clause to the dependent clause. Neither a dependent clause nor a changing-word subordinator will ever appear in a compound sentence. The compound sentence contains only independent clauses, two or more. With the compound sentence comes a myriad of opportunities to increase our arsenal of workable sentences. I have watched students move with confidence from writing the simple sentence to the complex sentence to the compound sentence. Composing sentences without knowing their structure wearies the strongest among us. And learning the various ways to write them improves writing skills and builds confidence.

The steps necessary to writing clear, concise compound sentences are easy to follow and fun to implement. First, learn a clear definition of the compound sentence. A compound sentence is a sentence that contains two or more independent clauses. Determining the kind of each clause is essential to correctly writing the compound sentence, and we have covered that subject well thus far. The question arises then as to what punctuation is needed between the two clauses.

At this point the fun begins. Four different punctuations can be written between independent clauses. The first and most frequent punctuation is (, and). One of the comma rules exists solely for the coordinate conjunction when it joins independent clauses. The rule is clear. Place a comma before (in front of) a coordinate conjunction when it joins independent clauses. FANBOYS surfaces again. FANBOYS is an acronym that helps us remember seven coordinate conjunctions: *for, and, nor, but, or, yet* and *so*. Whenever any one of these seven coordinate conjunctions is written between two independent clauses, a comma is placed in front of the conjunction. Let's enumerate the remaining three ways to punctuate compound sentences. It is of utmost importance to understand that we are talking about the punctuation that appears between independent clauses. The second most frequently used punctuation between independent clauses is the semicolon (;) all by itself. That's the mark that is equivalent to the equal sign (=) in mathematical equations. A third way to punctuate between two independent clauses is the semicolon followed by a conjunctive adverb followed by a comma. Some frequently used conjunctive adverbs are *consequently, furthermore, however, moreover, nonetheless, therefore, thus.*

The fourth and probably least common mark used to punctuate between clauses is the colon (:), the first cousin to the semicolon.

An illustration of the first punctuation rule for compound sentences is:

> Your wife Elizabeth will bear you a son, and you are to give him the name John. (Luke 1:13b)

The (, and) construction is our friend. It works like the equal sign in a mathematical equation and joins two clauses equal structurally. The grammatical structure of this sentence was chosen by the writer to assure that the reader understands the importance of the name John, which is equal to the unbelievable fact of an old woman having a baby. The structure actually begins hinting at the fact that this John is John the Baptist.

The complete verb in the first clause is *will bear*. Whenever editing a sentence always begin with the verb. The subject of *will bear* is *wife*. No changing-word subordinator appears in front of the subject-verb cluster. Therefore, we know that with no subordinator, the clause is independent. *Elizabeth* is in apposition (side by side or in close proximity) to *wife*; we call *Elizabeth* an appositive. The terms glossary of the *Simon and Schuster Handbook for Writers*, page 822, defines an *appositive* as "a word or group of words that renames a preceding noun or noun phrase: my favorite month, October."

Your is a pronoun, a possessive pronoun. It shows ownership like other possessive pronouns: *his, my, our, their*. Frequently possessive pronouns serve as adjectives, *his* cross, *my* prayer, *our* forgiveness, *their* release. In Luke 1:13b, the clause, *Your wife Elizabeth will bear you a son*, is independent. The next clause, *you are to give him the name John*, is also independent.

The verb in this clause is *are*. Don't fall into the trap of calling *to give* a verb. It isn't. It's an infinitive, one of the three verbals, which we will cover in chapter nine. The subject is *you*. The subject-verb cluster is *you are*, and there is no subordinator. The coordinate conjunction *and* joins the two clauses with the comma present. Note that in addition to the New International Version, the King James Version, the New American Standard Bible and the Revised Standard Version all join these clauses with (, and) between the two independent clauses. So the (, and) between independent clauses will always be correct. Get comfortable using this most frequently used punctuation when joining independent clauses.

Luke 2:9 gives an example of a compound sentence with three independent clauses. And the punctuation separating the clauses is exactly the same as in the previous passage (, and).

> An angel of the Lord appeared to them, and the glory of the Lord shone around them, and they were terrified.

The first two independent clauses are separated with the (, and). The subject-verb cluster in the first clause is *angel/appeared*. The subject-verb cluster in the second clause is *glory/shone*. The subject-verb cluster in the third clause is *they/were terrified*. This compound sentence, Luke 2:9, contains three independent clauses. Not one of the three clauses contains a changing-word subordinator in front of the subject-verb cluster. Therefore, all three clauses are independent. These two instances of punctuating with (, and) between clauses illustrate the following comma rule: place a comma before (in front of) a coordinate conjunction when that conjunction joins independent clauses.

Surely the world will not end if this rule is not obeyed every time. Some editors and some teachers, and perhaps some circumstances, may not require it. However, one of our goals in studying *Sacred Grammar* is to focus on sentence structure. I want the student of this text to know that a comma is inserted before a coordinate conjunction whenever it joins independent clauses. I am not wild about loading the page with commas; I prefer the opposite. But when your correct comma usage shows that you are clear on punctuating the compound sentence, that's one more step toward mastering sentence structure.

Luke 2:25b employs the comma/coordinate conjunction punctuation in yet another compound sentence. "He was waiting for the consolation of Israel, and the Holy Spirit was upon him."

This passage in Luke refers to Simeon, a righteous and devout follower of the Jewish law. The occasion is the presentation of the baby Jesus to the Lord. Simeon took the baby into his arms and blessed God, saying, "You are releasing your bondservant to depart in peace according to your word; for my eyes have seen your salvation, which you have prepared in the presence of all peoples, a light of revelation to the Gentiles, and the glory of your people Israel" (Luke 2:29-32, New American Standard Bible).

The subject-verb cluster in the first clause of Luke 2:25b, *He/was waiting*, has no changing-word subordinator. The clause with no subordinate conjunction or relative pronoun is independent. The subject-verb cluster with its complete clause reads, *the Holy Spirit was upon him*. Again, the only word in the clause in front of subject-verb cluster is the article *the*. The word *the* subordinates nothing; the clause is independent and is joined to the first clause by one of those FANBOYS coordinate conjunctions. The comma rule governing coordinate conjunctions comes into play, thus the comma before the (, *and*). I give examples of this form of punctuation because it is easily the most frequently used punctuation when writing the compound sentence. Luke's Gospel holds a goldmine of compound sentences.

Another way to punctuate the compound sentence is the semicolon (;). I ask my students to think of the semicolon as equivalent to the equal sign (=) in math. Although the semicolon is used most often in compound sentences, it may be used in other instances. But it always joins elements that are equal in structure. Had we placed a semicolon in place of the (, and) in Luke 1:13b, we would have been correct. These different ways to punctuate the compound sentence are interchangeable. They are all correct and offer flexibility to our writing.

The comma followed by *and* (, and) and the semicolon are always correct whenever they separate two independent clauses. But suppose a sentence has a third clause in addition to the two independent clauses. These two punctuations are still correct. Be sure to look inside the independent clause for a relative pronoun or a subordinate conjunction. Either would introduce a dependent clause and thereby make the sentence not compound but compound-complex. Don't let the semicolon throw you off. Let me give an example from Luke 1:51.

> He has performed mighty deeds with his arm; he has scattered those who are proud in their inmost thoughts.

The semicolon in this sentence is correct. However the sentence is not a compound sentence because it contains a third clause, inside one of the independent clauses, that happens to be a dependent clause. This verse, Luke 1:51, is a compound-complex sentence.

A compound sentence has two or more independent clauses—no dependent clause. But this verse concludes with a dependent clause, *who are proud in their inmost thoughts.* This sentence-ending clause begins with the relative pronoun *who*. Relative pronouns in front of the subject-verb cluster make the clause dependent. Note that in this sentence the relative pronoun *who* is the subject of the verb *are* and at the same time subordinates the clause making it dependent. The New International Version (NIV) correctly places no comma between the words *those* and *who*. Adding this dependent clause makes this a compound-complex sentence. Adding this clause in no way changes our punctuating with the semicolon (;) between the two independent clauses.

We cannot leave Luke 1:51 without talking about the Song of Mary, "The Magnificat," a sweet description of justice. While Simeon's song spoke of his longing for and expectancy of the coming Messiah, Mary's song, sung to a pregnant Elizabeth, captures the essence of the Kingdom of God, which would be fulfilled with the birth of her son.

> And Mary said: My soul glorifies in the Lord
> and my spirit rejoices in God my Saviour,
> for He has been mindful
> of the humble state of his servant.
> From now on all generations will call me blessed,
> For the Mighty One has done great things for me—
> holy is his name.
> His mercy extends to those who fear him,
> from generation to generation.
> He has performed mighty deeds with his arm;
> he has scattered those who are proud in their inmost thoughts.
> He has brought down rulers from their thrones
> but has lifted up the humble.
> He has filled the hungry with good things
> but has sent the rich away empty.
> He has helped his servant Israel,
> remembering to be merciful

to Abraham and his descendants forever,
even as he said to our fathers.
(Luke 1:46-55)

Look at Luke 2:36b: "She was very old; she had lived with her husband seven years after her marriage."

The semicolon (;) between these two independent clauses is vintage punctuation for a compound sentence. It gives a variety of choice for the writer. Be sure you understand that this sentence has only two independent clauses, two subject-verb clusters separated by the semicolon. The verse describes Anna, a prophetess of the tribe of Asher, always in the Temple, who witnessed the dedication of the baby Jesus to the Lord. She praised God and echoes the joy of the arrival of the Messiah.

Luke 8:10b quotes lines of poetry from Isaiah 6:9. The last part of this verse from Luke reads as follows:

Though seeing, they may not see; though hearing, they may not understand.

Again, these words form a compound sentence, two independent clauses. This verse shows the balance of the equal elements that are joined by the semicolon (;). We readily see that if these words were a mathematical equation, the semicolon could be replaced by an equal sign (=).

The verse is lifted from the parable of the four soils, which represents groups of hearers of the Gospel. The parallel images in the verse describe one of the different groups.

Like the American poet Walt Whitman, Isaiah, centuries earlier, wrote prose-like poetry. By prose like I mean that his poetry reads like sentences rather than structured poetry with rhyme and meter. Note the two independent clauses on either side of the semicolon. Another example of using the semicolon to separate independent clauses is found in the Song of Solomon 2:16.

My lover is mine and I am his; he browses among the lilies.

This verse contains three independent clauses. The first two short clauses are joined by the coordinate conjunction while the second and third clauses are joined by the semicolon. So the first two ways to join independent clauses are with the comma before a coordinate conjunction (, and) and with the semicolon all by itself.

A third way to join independent clauses introduces the use of the conjunctive adverb preceded by a semicolon and followed by a comma. A few of the frequently used conjunctive adverbs are *consequently*, *furthermore*, *however*, *therefore*, *thus* and *therefore*. This third form of punctuation introduces a rather sophisticated method that I recommend using sparingly in your writing. It furnishes even more variety, more possibilities when the writer faces the blank page. Try one right now on scratch paper. If you wrote something like "Jesus wept in the garden of Gethsemane; however, the disciples slept in the barn," your attempt is perfect. The large majority of the writing public does not know what you know about this compound sentence. Nor do they know that the semicolon avoids the usual error, the comma splice. I can tell you that the majority of freshmen writers in colleges across America would write the comma splice between the words *Gethsemane* and *however*. Now, you know better.

Recently, a student asked me to read his research paper. It had been graded and returned by a professor from a college far from where I teach. The grade and comments pleased the writer very much. The grade was A, but the comments addressed only the content of the paper. In a setting away from the student, I read the first few pages of his A paper. The information I read was above average, and the paper was essentially error free grammatically. However, the sameness of the sentence structure resulted in dullness. He had written mostly simple sentences with a sprinkling of compound sentences. Several complex sentences appeared, according to the writer, by accident.

According to the writer's own testimony, he had no knowledge of subordination or subordinate conjunctions or subordinate clauses. I told him he need not apologize. He needed to acquaint himself with the material in the text, *Sacred Grammar*. I asked him to rewrite the paper and bring it back to me after reviewing the four kinds of sentences. He did and his changes improved the paper. The old adage "variety is the spice of life" is not always true. However, it is true when we edit sentences. Long sentences that begin the same make for dull reading. I tell my students that just because they are eternal, their sentences do not have to be.

Let us review some of the sentence types we have covered thus far. Look at the different patterns of the following three sentences. Note especially the beginnings of the sentences, say, the first four or five words.

> Although Jesus wept in the garden, the disciples slept in the barn.

Jesus wept in the garden; the disciples slept in the barn.
Jesus wept in the garden; however, the disciples slept in the barn.

From your study in this text, you know that sentence number 1 is a complex sentence introduced by a dependent clause. *Although* is the changing-word subordinate conjunction. A comma follows this dependent clause because of the comma rule that states the following: place a comma after a long introductory clause or phrase. This is an introductory clause because it is a dependent clause and because it introduces an independent clause that follows it. The subject-verb cluster of the second clause is *disciples/slept*. The three steps of our clause test show us that there is a verb and a subject, but there is not a word-changing subordinator in front of *disciples*. The *disciples slept* clause is independent. And one independent clause with one or more dependent clauses builds a complex sentence.

Sentence number 2 features our old friend, the semicolon. I have stated before in this book that the average freshman writer does not use semicolons. Neither do other writers who are unsure and intimidated whenever they sit to write. The semicolon is learned best if it is treated like the equal sign in math: 6x = 36, x = 6. Those equal signs tell us that everything on one side of the equal sign is equal to everything on the other side of the equation, perhaps not precisely in content but certainly in structure. The semicolon (;) is exactly the same, joining two clauses structurally equal.

In sentence number 2 the first clause is independent. Again we apply the one-, two-, three-step clause test. You know those steps: verb, subject and word-changing subordinator. The subject-verb cluster in that first clause of sentence number 2 has no subordinator. Therefore the clause is independent. Note please that this first clause, although it opens the sentence, is not called introductory. It is not considered to be introducing the second clause because it is not dependent on or subordinate to that second clause. It could form its own sentence. Likewise, the second clause in sentence number 2 reads, "the disciples slept in the barn." The only word in front of the subject-verb cluster in this clause is the article *the*. There is no changing-word subordinator. The sentence is a compound sentence because it contains two or more independent clauses. I have said all of this in order to shine the spotlight on the semicolon (;) sitting so beautifully between the two independent clauses. Whenever you, the writer, have written two independent clauses together, back to back, you can punctuate with the semicolon. Understanding this one use of the semicolon removes you from that bewildered group who are afraid to use the semicolon at all. But a word of caution: don't overuse this new friend. Some of my students, upon learning this new way to write the compound sentence, will use it nonstop. Don't do that. As you become familiar and comfortable with its use, both in your writing and by noticing it elsewhere, you will begin to wield the semicolon with ever-increasing grace.

In sentence number 3 we branch out into the freedom of the compound sentence at its finest through the use of the conjunctive adverb. The conjunctive adverb never subordinates a clause. The third sentence above uses the popular conjunctive adverb *however*. That sentence reads, "Jesus wept in the garden; however, the disciples slept in the barn." We have simply added a conjunctive adverb followed by a comma (,). Learning this pattern will open up the opportunity for even greater freedom and variety in your writing and will carry any writer a long way toward excellence.

Learn the conjunctive adverb lists. Jeremiah the Hebrew prophet and St. Paul the apostle used *therefore* frequently. We can too. Be sure that you know a long list of conjunctive adverbs.

also	however	next
anyhow	incidentally	otherwise
anyway	indeed	similarly
besides	instead	still
consequently	likewise	then
finally	meanwhile	therefore
furthermore	moreover	thus
hence	nevertheless	

This list of conjunctive adverbs is quoted from page 68 of the fifteenth edition of *Hodges' Harbrace Handbook*. Write all these words on 3 × 5 index flash cards. *Hodges' Handbook* renders a valuable service on page 69 in its discussion on punctuating sentences with conjunctive adverbs. It states, "A comma used to set off a conjunctive adverb is sometimes omitted when there is no risk of misreading. The sea was usually hot; thus the coral turned white. No misreading is possible, so the comma can be omitted." We are not bound to using the comma every time; however, we must check for any possibility of misreading.

The New Well-Tempered Sentence by Karen Elizabeth Gordon should be at the fingertips of all writers whatever their skill level. On page 59 she summarizes the semicolon (;) as follows, "Semicolons, unlike commas, are separating only, when a period is a tougher break than what your sense demands." This telling word from Professor Gordon coincides with my concrete image of the equal sign in the mathematics equation. Both Hodges and Gordon are telling us that there exist many uses of the semicolon in addition to the punctuation in the middle of the compound sentence.

Putting closure on the discussion of the conjunctive adverb, *Hodges' Handbook* (69) lists fifteen transitional phrases that should be used since they behave as conjunctive adverbs.

Transitional Phrases

after all	even so	in fact
as a result	for example	in other words
at any rate	in addition	on the contrary
at the same	time in comparison	on the other hand
by the way	in contrast	that is

Each of the phrases functions exactly as a conjunctive adverb. My favorite conjunctive adverbs are *however*, *therefore* and *thus*. I could write the correct sentence, *However Jesus wept*. I could write the correct sentence, *Therefore Jesus wept*. Then I could substitute any one of the transitional phrases listed here. *At the same time Jesus wept* or *On the other hand Jesus wept* are perfectly correct sentences, because neither of these transitional phrases subordinates the clauses that follow.

In our Parts of Speech Chart, we introduced the Connector Tunnel that lists conjunctions and prepositions as connectors. At this point in this book we can review subordination by listing again a healthy group of subordinate conjunctions and relative pronouns. We must know these words, what they are called, what they do and how they differ from each other. The *Hodges' Harbrace Handbook*, fifteenth edition, lists the following subordinate conjunctions (41):

after	now that
although	once
as	provided (that)
as if	since
as though	so that
because	though
before	unless
even if	until
even though	when, whenever
how	where, wherever
if	whether
in case	while
in that	no matter how
in so far as	

Please note well, *nota bene*, that failing to write these different groups of words on flash cards is failing to gain full benefit of your study. Writing them on flash cards and failing to memorize them wastes time and paper. Memorizing them after writing them on flash cards but not using them effectively in your written work is a missed opportunity. Savor the joy of putting hand to the plow. Plowing is difficult work, but it yields life-giving crops. Your diligence in learning these various groups of words and what they do will reap a harvest of good writing for you. Captives of the computer, allergic to paper, are excused from the archaic 3 × 5 index cards *only* if a substitute method of learning has been discovered.

Each of the subordinate conjunctions listed above is to be learned as a part of speech that changes an independent clause to a dependent clause. This change, as you know, is called subordination. The words in this list are subordinate conjunctions only if they are followed by a subject-verb cluster. Some of the words in the list can function as other parts of speech. For example, the first word in the list, *after*, can function as several parts of speech. If we write, *after the flood*, we have written a prepositional phrase. Prepositional phrases begin with prepositions. Here the beginning word, *after*, is a preposition. If it appears in front of a subject-verb cluster, it's a subordinate conjunction, and the clause that has been subordinated is dependent, needing an independent clause in order to form a sentence. It is clear why we call subordinators, both subordinate conjunctions and relative pronouns, changing-word subordinators. They are words that change the clauses following them from independent to dependent.

The other group of subordinators that should be reviewed here is the relative pronoun. I ask my students to learn the basic seven relative pronouns. There may be some variations of a few of these words, but the basic seven suffice. They are as follows:

> that
> what
> whatever
> which
> who
> whom
> whose

These changing-word subordinators (relative pronouns) frequently are written after independent clauses to form complex sentences. Look at the following sentences. Each one begins with an independent clause followed by a dependent clause. The dependent clause in each sentence has been made dependent by the relative pronoun that changes the clause from independent to dependent.

> Christ is the one who forgives sins.
>
> Now Ehud made a double edged-sword about three and a half feet long, which he strapped to his right thigh under his clothing. (Judges 3:16)
>
> He had a thousand goats and three thousand sheep, which he was shearing in Carmel. (1 Samuel 25:2)

In the first sentence above, the clause *Christ is the one* contains the subject-verb cluster. No changing-word subordinator appears in front of the subject-verb cluster, *Christ is*. Therefore, the clause is independent and gives the possibility of having a sentence. The next clause *who forgives sins* contains the changing-word relative pronoun *who*. The *who forgives sins* clause is, therefore, dependent. The dependent clause tells which *one* Christ is—*the one who forgives sins.*

In Judges 3:16 the *sword* is the noun in the independent clause modified by the relative clause *which he strapped to his right thigh under his clothing*.

I have discussed subordinate conjunctions and relative pronouns at this juncture in order to further differentiate the compound sentence from the complex sentence. As stated earlier, no compound sentence will ever contain a subordinate conjunction or a relative pronoun.

It's review time. Lock yourself into the following review questions. You don't want to proceed without a clear understanding of the answers. Make as many flash cards (the 3 × 5, old friends) as you need to get them memorized.

Review Questions for Chapter Five: The Compound Sentence

1. Define a compound sentence.
2. Define subordination.
3. What two parts of speech subordinate clauses?
4. Why do compound sentences contain no subordinators?
5. Name the four ways of separating independent clauses in a compound sentence.
6. What is the significance of the acronym FANBOYS?
7. State the comma rule that applies to coordinate conjunctions.
8. What is the most used punctuation between independent clauses?
9. What is the least used punctuation between independent clauses?
10. The semicolon (;) between independent clauses resembles what mark in a mathematical equation?
11. Is the compound sentence limited to the number of independent clauses it may have?
12. What is the most frequent comma usage error?
13. Why do many writers avoid using the semicolon?
14. In this lesson what Hebrew prophet is likened to American poet Walt Whitman?
15. The first two ways to punctuate between independent clauses are (, and) and the semicolon. What part of speech is used to implement the third choice of punctuation mentioned in this chapter?
16. Sameness of sentence structure brings what result?
17. Write the comma rule that addresses introductory clauses or phrases.
18. Do conjunctive adverbs ever subordinate clauses?

19. Can a conjunctive adverb ever be a changing-word subordinator?
20. List twenty (20) subordinate conjunctions.
21. List twenty (20) conjunctive adverbs.
22. List seven (7) relative programs.
23. Can the words *after* and *before* function as different parts of speech?
24. When are *after* and *before* always subordinate conjunctions?
25. List five (5) coordinate conjunctions.

SIX

The Compound-Complex Sentence

    The compound-complex sentence concludes our discussion of the four kinds of sentences according to structure. And the structure of a sentence depends only on its clauses. A clause is a group of related words that contains a subject (noun or pronoun) and a verb. In *Sacred Grammar* we have called the subject and its verb the subject-verb cluster. A subject-verb cluster forms a clause. The only other group of words that we identify in this book is the phrase, which is defined as a group of related words that does not contain a subject and a verb. It's just that simple.

    If no independent clause exists in a group of words, that group of words is not a sentence. Whenever we have a clause, that group of words is either an independent clause or a dependent clause. The four kinds of sentences structurally are determined and defined by the number of and kinds of clauses contained in the sentence.

    A simple sentence is a sentence that contains only one independent clause. A single independent clause is a simple sentence, all on its own. Certainly, every sentence conveys a complete thought; however, that definition for a simple sentence does not provide a structural definition. From the single independent clause simple sentence, we move easily into more complex constructions.

    The complex sentence is a logical expansion of the simple sentence because we expand, if you please, the definition of the simple sentence. Therefore, we define the complex sentence as the sentence that contains only one independent clause and one or more dependent clauses.

    The compound sentence we examined thoroughly in chapter five. The compound sentence like the simple sentence builds on the independent clause. Only independent clauses appear in compound sentences. The compound sentence is a sentence that contains two or more independent clauses. The compound sentence will never contain a dependent clause or any one of the changing-word subordinators (subordinate conjunctions or relative pronouns).

I ask my students to learn, in order, the first three kinds of sentences according to structure: simple, complex, compound. Both the simple sentence and the complex sentence contain only one independent clause. Then moving to the definition of the compound sentence, we have only two or more independent clauses—no dependent clause at all. Finally, the fourth kind of sentence, the compound-complex sentence, as its name implies, contains the combination of a compound sentence and a complex sentence: two or more independent clauses and one or more dependent clauses.

Knowledge of the different combinations of the four kinds of sentences is not only easy to grasp but also rewarding to use. It's freeing, not binding. I am not putting you under the burden of memorization; I am lifting you from the haze of ambiguity. I have seen dozens of good writers work in the dark. They didn't know the structure of their sentences; they really didn't know "compound from dog pound." (Remember my good student who, long ago, taught me that silly expression.) But when these same writers learn that two independent clauses form a compound sentence, they note that the punctuation between the clauses could not be a comma, and they avoid the dreaded comma splice. Having learned structure, like any good carpenter, these students now know how to build. Chapter seven, which focuses on the decorating of sentences, further illustrates the clear structural differences among them.

Let us go now to the investigation of several compound-complex sentences from the Bible. This is an enjoyable exercise. During the reign of good King Josiah, the Lord spoke to Jeremiah concerning the unfaithfulness of the sister nations, Israel and Judah. The following sentence is a compound-complex sentence. Be sure to grasp a clear understanding why it is compound-complex. In the (NIV) Jeremiah 3:7 reads,

> I thought
> that after she had done all this
> she would return to me
> but
> she did not,

and
her unfaithful sister Judah saw it.

In the sentence above, I have separated the clauses on the page in order to look at each clause independently of the others. *I thought* is an independent clause as surely as *Jesus wept* (John 11:35) is an independent clause. There is no changing-word subordinator in front of *I thought*. Therefore this two-word clause is an independent clause. Had the writer ended the sentence after this two-word clause, the sentence would be a simple sentence. The next clause in this sentence reads *that after she had done all this*. The verb in this clause is *had done* and the subject is *she*. In front of this subject-verb cluster sits one of our old friends, the relative pronoun *that*. The relative pronoun makes the clause dependent.

In chapter seven, "Decorating Sentences," we will draw a circle around all subordinators, subordinate conjunctions and relative pronouns. So far in this sentence from the book of Jeremiah, we have seen an independent clause, *I thought*, and a dependent clause, *that after she had done all this*. Three independent clauses follow:

She would return to me
but
she did not;
and
her unfaithful sister saw it.

The last three clauses are independent since not one of the three subject-verb clusters has a subordinate conjunction or a relative pronoun in front of it. Be sure that you understand fully this last sentence. Now, we simply count all the clauses and determine the kinds of each of the clauses that we have in the entire sentence. Why don't you do this for practice right now? Go back to the full sentence and check out the five clauses. We will scrutinize clauses in the next chapter that covers the decoration of sentences. But for now please ferret out the details of this one on your own.

Why do we place so much emphasis on the different clauses in these sentences? It's about editing. Unless I know that a dependent clause written alone is a fragment, I might be prone to write one as a sentence. When my students see their sentences in segments, their writing improves. Learning subordination, independent versus dependent clauses, and subject-verb clusters is not just about grammar; it's about editing sentences. I want you to be able to take apart any sentence that you have written. These investigations of the sentences are invaluable. Let's look at another compound-complex sentence.

1 Kings 18 describes a long drought when King Ahab ruled the Northern Kingdom of Israel. The drought has resulted in a devastating famine. 1 Kings 18:2b, 3a reports with a compound-complex sentence the following:

> Now the famine was severe in Samaria,
> and
> Ahab had summoned Obadiah
> who was in charge of his palace.

This sentence from 1 Kings is an example of the compound-complex sentence at its best. By that I mean that it is correct, and its pattern is used often by good writers. The verb in the first clause is *was* and its subject is *famine*. The subject-verb cluster is *famine/was*. Let's examine what we have. Remembering our clause test from earlier in this book, we learned that our three steps are locate the verb first, locate the subject of the verb second and the third step is to determine if the subject-verb cluster has a subordinator in front of it. Two words sit in front of the subject-verb cluster, *now the*. I mention my students because the majority of them, by this time in their journey through *Sacred Grammar*, have memorized the list of subordinate conjunctions and the list of relative pronouns. Neither list contains the word *now*. And certainly neither list contains the word *the*. That all-important clause test asks three questions. Is a verb present? Does that verb have a subject? And is a subordinator present in front of that subject-verb cluster? If the first two answers are *yes*, we have a clause. If the third answer is *yes*, the clause is dependent. If the answer is *no* to the third question, the clause is independent because no subordinator has made the clause dependent.

Before we look at the second clause, let's look at the (, and) that joins the first two clauses. Why this comma? The comma is necessary because there is a comma rule that requires it to be there. You know the rule: place a comma (,) before a coordinate conjunction when it joins two independent clauses. The next clause *Ahab had summoned Obadiah* is an independent clause. It has no changing-word subordinator in front of the subject-verb cluster. Two independent clauses followed by a relative (dependent) clause made dependent by the relative pronoun *who* form the compound-complex sentence. The responsibility here is to understand clearly how the three clauses form this particular kind of sentence. If you are clear on this, you can write with confidence a sentence like it. Now let's go to the Gospel of Mark 10:31.

But many who are first will be last, and the last (will be) first.

Here we come upon our old friend *who* inside the sentence forming a dependent clause. The dependent clause is formed by the three interior words *who are first*. What three words in the verse form the dependent clause? The three words *who are first* form the dependent clause. What word subordinates the clause? The relative pronoun *who* subordinates the clause, making this dependent clause a relative clause. Can this clause serve as both the subject of the verb and the subordinator of the clause at the same time? Yes, the relative pronoun *who* in this sentence is both the subject of the verb and the subordinator of the clause. Also, note the first word in this sentence, the coordinate conjunction *but*. Verse translations from the King James Version (1611) to the New International Version frequently begin with *and* and *but*. Review the structure of this compound-complex sentence from Mark 10:31 above. I place this verse here, hoping to keep you on your toes. It is compound-complex, not complex, in spite of the *but* at the beginning of the verse and the dependent clause in the middle of an independent clause.

In the seventh chapter of Mark's Gospel, Jesus has the opportunity to heal a man who is deaf and dumb. Mark 7:32 reads,

> There some people brought to him a man
> who was deaf and could hardly talk,
> and
> they begged him to place his hand on the man.

The first eight words of the sentence form an independent clause. The subject-verb cluster is *people/brought* with no subordinator in front of the subject of the verb. The next seven words, *who was deaf and could hardly talk*, form a dependent clause whose subject is both the subordinator (relative pronoun) and the subject of the verbs *was* and *could . . . talk*. The last clause in the sentence is independent and is joined to the rest of the sentence by the familiar coordinate conjunction with a comma in front of it. Note that this punctuation is correct even though a dependent clause is written between the two independent clauses. The dependent clause in this sentence sits between two independent clauses. In our sentence just before this one, the *who* clause came at the end of the sentence after two independent clauses.

Compound-complex sentences appear in all kinds of good writing. The account of the shipwreck in Acts 27:27-44 contains a whopper of a compound-complex sentence in verse thirty-nine (Acts 27:39). There is no need to learn or memorize sentence patterns. What must be learned is the recognition of each clause and how it fits with those joining it. The verse that follows has many clauses. No writer wants to pen too many sentences like this one. However, for our need to see a variety of sentences, this one serves our purpose. Identify the five different clauses in the following verse from Acts:

> When daylight came
> they did not recognize the land,
>   but
> they saw a bay with a sandy beach
> where they decided to run the ship aground
> if they could.

Lay hold of what you have learned and walk through this sentence. For a fun exercise write this sentence in your *Sacred Grammar* notebook. Go back through each clause and draw two straight lines beneath each verb and one straight line beneath each subject of each verb. You should find five clauses. Then identify each clause by locating the three clauses that have subordinators in front of the subject. Draw a circle around those three subordinators. Place [brackets] around the five complete clauses. Be sure to label each clause above its verb as either independent (ind.) or dependent (dep.). Clauses one (1), four (4) and five (5) begin respectively with the changing-word subordinators *when*, *where* and *if*. Those three clauses are dependent; each is made dependent by its changing-word subordinator. Clauses two (2) and three (3) are independent clauses. Respectively, their subject-verb clusters are *they/did . . . recognize* and *they/saw*. No subordinator (subordinate conjunction or relative pronoun) appears in front of the subject-verb clusters in clauses two (2) or three (3). Of course, both of those clauses are independent clauses. Again, count the total number of clauses. There are five. Two are independent clauses, and three are dependent clauses. By definition this sentence is a compound-complex sentence. It contains two or more independent clauses and one or more dependent clauses. This exercise with this verse (Acts 27:39) prepares us for chapter seven that explores how to decorate the four kinds of sentences.

Review Questions for Chapter Six: The Compound-Complex Sentence

1. Name the four kinds of sentences according to structure.
2. In this text, *Sacred Grammar*, what precisely do we mean by "structure"?
3. Define a clause.
4. What are the names of the two primary segments or groups of words that we use in this grammar text?
5. Define a simple sentence.
6. Define a complex sentence.
7. Define a compound sentence.
8. Define a compound-complex sentence.
9. Why do expressions such as "a complete thought" and "convey an idea" fail to define a sentence?
10. Identify the dependent clause in Jeremiah 3:7.
11. Name the subordinator (subordinate conjunction or relative pronoun) in Jeremiah 3:7.
12. Define a fragment.
13. Why is it a good practice to learn the definitions of sentences in the following order: simple, complex, compound, compound-complex?
14. Write a simple sentence.
15. Write a complex sentence.
16. Write a compound sentence.
17. Write a compound-complex sentence.
18. List fifteen (15) subordinate conjunctions.
19. List seven (7) relative pronouns.
20. Write the three steps helpful to determine whether a clause is dependent or independent.
21. At the close of chapter six, we begin to introduce the decorating of sentences. What marks do we write beneath verbs and subjects? What do we write around subordinators?

SEVEN

Decorating Sentences

In chapters three through six, we investigated the four kinds of sentences according to structure. They are simple, complex, compound and compound-complex. A sentence that contains only one independent clause is a simple sentence. A sentence that contains only one independent clause and at least one or more dependent clauses is a complex sentence. A sentence that contains two or more independent clauses is a compound sentence. A sentence that contains two or more independent clauses and one or more dependent clauses is a compound-complex sentence. Understanding these four structures is easy once we know and understand the two kinds of clauses, the independent clause and the dependent clause.

The first grammatical nugget that we will learn to notice in decorating sentences is our old friend, the subject-verb cluster. Wherever a subject-verb cluster is written, we have a clause. You have learned that an independent clause written alone is a sentence. Also, I've asked you to learn one of the best definitions of a simple sentence—one independent clause. The decorating of sentences enables the writer to edit sentences beginning with the subject-verb cluster and moving out from there toward the beginning and the end of the sentence. By learning to decorate sentences many students in my classes have become comfortable editing their compositions and research papers.

Diagramming versus Decorating

Many decades ago a good English teacher in grade school attempted to teach me to diagram sentences. I did not enjoy diagramming sentences then, and I do not relish it now. Diagramming draws lines and things down the page below the written sentence if I recall correctly. And if your teacher wants you to diagram sentences, I want you to diagram sentences. Decorating sentences is not diagramming sentences. Diagramming sentences is vertical in that it moves down the page, repeating the words in the sentence. Decorating sentences, on the other hand, is horizontal in that it marks the various parts of the sentence as the words appear on the page. I teach decorating as a step toward editing. It is my creation, and for more years than I care to remember, I've watched with pleasure as students profit from the procedure. Now let's decorate.

We use a total of eight different marks to decorate sentences: two straight lines under the complete verb, one straight line under the subject of the verb, three straight lines under the direct object of the verb, four straight lines under an indirect object, a wavy line under a complement, a circle or oval around a word or words that subordinate a clause, (parentheses) around phrases and [brackets] around complete clauses.

After we make all our marks in our sentence, we identify each clause by writing "ind" above the verb in each independent clause and by writing "dep" above the verb in each dependent clause. The last step in decorating a sentence is the writing of "simple," "complex," "compound" or "compound-complex" in the margin to the left of that sentence. You are perfectly free to use any abbreviations that might suit you. It's fun. My students find themselves not only profiting from the exercise of decorating, but also actually enjoying the experience.

Decorating in Action: the Book of John

Let's revisit John 11:35. The entire verse reads, "Jesus wept."
Decorating this verse is a piece of cake. Two straight lines are written under *wept* while one straight line is written under the subject, *Jesus*. Those

are always the first two steps in decorating, but step number three is most important. After locating the verb and its subject, determine if there is a word or group of words (before) in front of the subject that subordinates the clause. Only two groups of words do this, subordinate conjunctions and relative pronouns. We have spoken of the clause test. This is the clause test. Check for a word that makes an independent clause dependent. A dependent clause written all by its lonesome is not a sentence. Grammar books and English teachers call this a fragment, something we want to avoid. That's an impostor, a fragment posing as a sentence.

Go again to John 11:35. Suppose I write on the classroom board, *While Jesus wept*. Is this a sentence or a fragment? The subordinate conjunction, *while*, makes this otherwise independent clause dependent. It cannot stand alone. Suppose I write on the board, *However, Jesus wept*. Do I have a sentence or a fragment? Knowing that *however* is a conjunctive adverb helps us to know that *However, Jesus wept* is an independent clause. It can stand alone as a sentence.

An independent clause written alone is always a simple sentence. Suppose John 11:35 read *Jesus wept over the sins of Jerusalem*. We still have a simple sentence because we still have only one independent clause. The words *over the sins* and *of Jerusalem* form two prepositional phrases in a row. The Parts of Speech Chart in chapter one teaches that a preposition is a word that joins its object to the rest of the sentence. Therefore, (parentheses) are placed around the two prepositional phrases, and [brackets] surround the first and last words of the complete clause: [*Jesus wept* (*over the sins*) (*of Jerusalem*).] Get in the habit of enclosing the complete clause with brackets.

When decorating sentences do not leave any of the words within a clause unbracketed. The only word not enclosed inside the brackets is a connecting word between the two clauses. A subordinate conjunction or relative pronoun (such as *if* or *which*) that makes a clause dependent is considered part of that clause and so should be placed inside the brackets, with the circle drawn around it. A coordinate conjunction or conjunctive adverb that joins two independent clauses (such as *and* or *but*) is not considered part of either clause, and therefore is left outside the brackets.

There is often the temptation to leave words that are part of a clause dangling out in space undecorated. Don't do it. The purpose of decorating sentences is to examine every detail. On scratch paper or in your *Sacred Grammar* notebook, write a few simple sentences. Start with *Jesus wept*. Decorate your sentences by underlining the verb and subject and by placing brackets around the entire clause. Remember that a simple sentence is one independent clause, and every word from first to last will be inside the brackets unless it is not a part of either clause. For example, neither coordinate conjunctions nor conjunctive adverbs that sit between clauses would be inside the brackets. A *but* or a *however* written at the beginning of a sentence would be written inside the brackets of a decorated sentence. Write enough sentences to include a few prepositional phrases.

Deeper Practice with Decorating: The Book of Luke

After you have written and decorated three or four of your own sentences, tackle the following sentence for fun and for practice. You are underlining each verb two times; find the subject of the verb and underline it one time. Any phrases such as prepositional phrases will be enclosed within parentheses. A phrase now and always is defined as a group of related words that does not contain a subject and a verb. If you haven't thought about subjects and verbs for a while, remember that every subject of every verb has to be a noun or a pronoun. Not one of the other seven parts of speech could correctly serve as a subject of a verb. The following sentence contains only one independent clause. Remember to write "Simple" in the left margin of this sentence with only one independent clause.

Please decorate Luke 4:22a:

All spoke well of him and were amazed at the gracious words that came from his lips.

[And no one dared (to ask him any more questions).] (Luke 20:40) Simple

These are but two of hundreds of sentences in the Holy Scriptures that hint at the personality of Jesus. Please see the excitement before and after these spicy verses. As a man, this Jesus of Nazareth fascinates all who might scrutinize him carefully.

Decorating a sentence, among other things, determines the number of clauses in the sentence and whether they are independent or dependent. In Luke 20:40, one of the verses above, there is only one verb, *dared*. Its subject is the word *one*. After locating the subject-verb cluster, we move to step three in the clause test: is there a changing-word subordinator, a subordinate conjunction or relative pronoun in front of the subject and verb? A subordinator in front of the subject-verb cluster makes the clause dependent. If no subordinator appears in front of the subject-verb cluster, the clause is independent.

I cannot overemphasize the importance of applying this clause test when decorating sentences. First, this little test tells us if we have a clause or a fragment. Almost every verse in the Bible is a sentence. Knowing why Luke 20:40 qualifies as a simple sentence begins our journey into editing. Only two words appear in front of the subject and verb; they are *and* and *no*. Checking our lists of subordinate conjunctions and relative pronouns, we find that neither *and* nor *no* appears. No subordinator is present; therefore, we have one independent clause. And no other subject-verb cluster appears in the sentence, so the sentence is simple, having only one independent clause. Look again at the first two words, *and* and *no*. The word *no*, an adjective, modifies the noun *one*. The first word in the sentence is *and*, a coordinate conjunction, the second word in the FANBOYS acronym.

Let me have my say again about *and* beginning a sentence. It's correct whenever Luke writes it in his Gospel. It's correct whenever you write it in your essays. It's correct whenever Harold Bloom writes *and* as the first word in his sentences. It's correct whenever Martin Luther King, Jr., speaks it in his speeches. Please believe me, beginning sentences with coordinate conjunctions, especially *and* and *but,* can make for good writing. And it is practiced judiciously by excellent writers.

Lets again place Luke 20:40 on the page fully decorated; it begins with the coordinate conjunction *and*.

Simple sentence [And no one dared (to ask him any more questions.)]

The coordinate conjunction as the first word of a sentence links that sentence in meaning to the one preceding it. Coordinate conjunctions *for, and, nor, but, or, yet* and *so* (FANBOYS) join equals. This is the reason that beginning a sentence with *and* or *but* is perfectly correct and effective when appropriate.

Some of my students are tempted to say that *to ask him* is a verb. These words actually form a verbal phrase, which is built from the infinitive *to ask*. Verbals and verbal phrases act as nouns, not verbs, so in Luke 20:40, *to ask him* is an infinitive phrase that acts as the direct object of the verb *dared*. Don't worry. In later chapters we will learn about the three types of verbals (gerunds, participles and infinitives), as well as more about verbs and direct objects. In decorating sentences we write three straight lines under direct objects. The direct object answers the question, what word or words receive the action of the verb? Only action verbs have objects that receive action. More information on verbs will appear in our next chapter.

So far in this chapter we have introduced five of the eight marks that we use in decorating sentences. The verb has two straight lines beneath it. The subject of the verb (always a noun or pronoun) has one line beneath it. If there is a phrase (prepositional, infinitive, etc.), parentheses surround it. [Brackets] enclose the entire clause. Let's review: beneath verbs, two straight lines; beneath subjects, one straight line; beneath direct objects, three straight lines; beneath indirect objects, four straight lines, beneath predicate complements, one wavy line; around phrases, parentheses; around clauses, brackets.

More Decorating: Kings, Ecclesiastes, Daniel and back to John

Upon finishing this chapter on decorating sentences, you should have all eight of these marks used in decorating written on 3 × 5 flash cards as well as in your *Sacred Grammar* notebook. Each of the eight marks must be learned and used in order to advance your skills as an editor. That's where we want to get.

Again let's go over the five marks we have covered and then let's add the remaining three to our arsenal. Subjects are underlined once and verbs twice. If the verb is an action verb, it can have a direct object. Direct objects of verbs are marked with three straight lines beneath the word or words that form the direct object of the verb. Again, the direct object receives the action of the verb. Look at the direct objects found in the following verses of scripture. You might want to decorate the entire sentence in each of the four examples from the Bible. If you exercise this option please write the verses in your *Sacred Grammar* notebook.

1. So the king sent a third captain with his fifty men. (2 Kings 1:13a)

The word *captain* answers the question, what word receives the action of the action verb? The action verb is *sent*. The king *sent* what? The answer is *captain*, the direct object of the verb. Checking for the kind of clause, we look at the word or words in front of the subject-verb cluster. The only word in front of the subject in this sentence is the word *so*. Checking our word lists we find that *so* is neither a subordinate conjunction nor a relative pronoun. The clause then is independent. Note that *so* is in our FANBOYS acronym of coordinate conjunctions. Therefore, *so* beginning this sentence is the same as *and* or *but* beginning a sentence. It is perfectly correct.

If you decorated 2 Kings 1:13a, the last four words, *with his fifty men*, would be surrounded by parentheses as a prepositional phrase. Now that we are investigating sentences more intensely, we can ask about prepositional phrases. Prepositional phrases act as modifiers—either adjectives or adverbs. The phrase *with his fifty men* modifies the noun *captain*. A word or a phrase that describes a noun or a pronoun is an adjective. This four-word prepositional phrase is an adjective. Some of my students find it helpful to identify the kind of phrase as well as stating the particular part of speech. The next verse follows the same pattern as 2 Kings 1:13a. Please decorate it for your *Sacred Grammar* notebook.

2. I saw the tears of the oppressed. (Eccles. 4:1b)

The action verb *saw*, with its pronoun subject *I*, has as its direct object the word, *tears*. In this sentence *tears* is a direct object of the verb because the verb shows action. Learn now that direct objects are objects of action verbs only. Linking verbs or any form of the verb *to be* (*am, are, is, was* and *were*) do not have objects following them. The prepositional phrase *of the oppressed* tells us about *tears*. What *tears* or whose *tears*? The word *tears* is a noun, and adjectives describe nouns. Again, just as in the previous sentence we have a prepositional phrase functioning as an adjective. You want to note this usage in your decoration just above the phrase. Be sure to state in the margin that both the first two sentences from scripture are simple sentences.

3. He changes times and seasons; he sets up kings and deposes them. (Dan. 2:21)

All three verbs in this compound sentence are action verbs, and each is followed by a direct object that receives the *action* of its action verb. In the first clause the action verb *changes* begs to have a direct object. So we ask our direct object question, what word or words receive the action of the verb? *He changes* what or whom? In this verse, the answer to our question gives us a compound direct object, *times* and *seasons*. *He changes times* and *He changes seasons*. The second clause contains two direct objects, one per verb. The word *kings* receives the action of the verb *sets (up)*, and the clause ends with the pronoun *them* as the direct object of the verb *deposes. He deposes them.*

Look back now at the first clause. Why is it independent? This clause test tells us that the verb is *changes,* and its subject is *he*. No word appears in front of the subject-verb cluster; the clause is independent. The second clause also has no word to subordinate the clause, so it is independent. Two independent clauses form a compound sentence.

We decorate this sentence with a set of brackets around each complete clause. No word in this twelve-word sentence would be left outside the brackets. Be sure to write three straight lines under each of the four direct objects.

4. Then they hurled insults at him. (John 9:28a)

Let's walk once more through the steps we use to decorate sentences. Underline the verb with two straight lines. Underline the subject of the verb with one straight line. Run the clause test. Determine if there is a word in front of the clause that makes the clause dependent. This sentence gives trouble to some of my students. The trouble begins when they confuse the word *then* with the word *when*. *Then* is not a subordinate conjunction; it's an adverb that modifies the verb *hurled*. *Then* does not subordinate the clause *they hurled*; it simply answers the question, when did they hurl?

This clause is independent and is a simple sentence. The direct object is clearly the word *insults*. What did they *hurl? They hurled insults.* The tiny prepositional phrase *at him* functions as an adverb telling the direction of the hurling. Get in the habit of noting how sentences begin—the ones you write as well as the ones you read. The beginning word or words of each clause tell if the clause is independent or dependent. The first four words of the sentences, say, of any given paragraph help determine variety and flow. This is one of many reasons why subordination is necessary to understand and to use if we are to achieve variety and quality in our sentences.

We have looked at direct objects in four verses from the Bible. Believe it or not almost everyone who learns direct objects wants to learn indirect objects as well—what they are and what they do. But then my students fret over them. Fortunately, I am able to relieve their vexation quickly since indirect objects are easy to grasp. First, there is no indirect object without a direct object. Also, the placement of the indirect object remains constant. An indirect object always follows the verb and comes before the direct object. It sits between them. Finally, I teach my students that the indirect object must be a noun or a pronoun, and that it usually answers the question *for whom* or *to whom*. In decorating we draw four straight lines beneath indirect objects. I want you to learn them, but I want you to know that they take care of themselves in your writing. Note the following examples for your comfort:

1. I gave a Bible.

Bible is the direct object of the action verb *gave* with the pronoun *I* serving as the subject of the verb. I gave what? I gave a *Bible*. This simple little sentence has no indirect object. Let's rewrite the sentence and give it one.

2. I gave my son a Bible.
   Decorating this sentence we discover the words *my son* sitting between the verb and its direct object. *My son* answers the question to whom the Bible was given? And thus *son* is the indirect object. Notice also that all indirect objects and all direct objects are in the objective case, the key word here being object.

   The man said, "The woman you put here with me—she **gave** me some fruit from the tree, and I ate it." (Gen. 3:12)

The word *me* is the indirect object answering the question, to whom did she give the fruit? *Fruit* is the direct object. *Fruit* is what *she* gave. The indirect object is always positioned between the verb and its direct object. In order for a sentence to have an indirect object, there must also be a direct object.

Predicate Nouns and Predicate Adjectives

The next mark used to decorate sentences is the wavy line that indicates *predicate complements*. The wavy line is written beneath *predicate nouns* and *predicate adjectives*, which are both *predicate complements*.

The word *complement,* spelled with two *e*'s, means to complete. A *predicate noun* is a noun in the predicate that renames the subject, while a *predicate adjective* is an adjective in the predicate that describes the subject. Example of a *predicate noun: Jesus is the Messiah.* Example of a *predicate adjective: Jeremiah is indomitable. Indomitable* is an adjective that follows the verb and modifies the subject *Jeremiah.* Why not look up *indomitable* in your dictionary to see what kind of man this prophet might have been.

We discuss the complement here for several reasons. One, it is often confused with direct objects. We must learn the difference in the two, but more importantly the reason for the difference between the complement and the direct object. A second reason I teach complements and direct objects together is because the position in the sentence is similar. Both follow the verb and are often both close to the verb.

A direct object follows an action verb. The action verb is frequently listed in dictionaries as a *transitive* verb. Transitive is indicated in the dictionary by v.t. or tr. A transitive verb in a sentence carries its action from the subject to another person, place or thing, which is then called a direct object. Every action verb can be transitive *or* intransitive. That is, the verb is transitive or intransitive according to its relationship to other words in the sentence. If the verb is intransitive (*not* transitive), it may be followed by a complement, not a direct object.

Let's take a moment to examine a few examples that will show the difference between direct objects and complements, predicate nouns or predicate adjectives.

1. God loves mankind.

In this sentence the verb *loves* is a transitive verb, and *mankind* is its direct object. Direct objects follow transitive verbs and receive the action of the verb. Complements follow intransitive verbs. *Webster's New Universal Unabridged Dictionary* defines an intransitive verb as "a verb that indicates a complete action without being accompanied by a direct object, as *sit* or *lie,* and, in English, that does not form a passive." Decorating this sentence we would write three straight lines under the word *mankind,* the direct object, because it receives the action or "love" of the action verb. But look at the difference in the following verb, which is intransitive, not transitive.

2. God is love.

The verb *is* is a form of the verb *to be*. It is intransitive and cannot have an object. The subject of the verb is *God*, and the noun *love* is the complement, the *predicate noun*. A *predicate noun* renames the subject of the verb. A *predicate adjective* modifies or describes the subject of the verb.

Sacred Grammar states repeatedly that nouns and pronouns in sentences have case. The word *mankind* in sentence number one, above, is in the objective case. The three cases in English are subjective (subjects and words joined to the subject), objective (the object of verbs, prepositions, verbals, etc.) and possessive (nouns and pronouns that show ownership). All nouns that are *predicate nouns* are in the subjective case because they rename the subject of the verb. They are not the objects, and certainly not direct objects, of anything. In our third case, an apostrophe (') must be present in every noun in the possessive case. And pronouns in English by nature change in the different cases, such as *me* and *my*. It would be helpful to revisit chapter two in this text, "The Case for the Three Cases."

3. God is merciful.

The word *merciful* is a complement, a predicate adjective. In this sentence the adjective *merciful* describes the subject, *God*. Some elements of grammar, say, indirect objects, take care of themselves. Complements do not.

Let me explain. Suppose you call my cell phone. You have never called me before; therefore, you are not sure who has answered your call. I say, "Hello." You say, "May I speak to Jim Beaty?" I reply, "This is he." This sentence is correct. Do you know why? Can you explain why "This is he" is correct and why "This is him" is incorrect? The reason "This is he" is correct is the complement *he*. The verb *is* cannot be followed with an object or an objective form of the pronoun. Any form of the verb "to be" is a linking verb, an intransitive verb. In this case it renames the subject with the pronoun *he*. I just wrote that complements do not take care of themselves. I simply mean that complements that are pronouns must be written in the subjective case form, every time. The pronouns *he*, *him* and *his* are intrinsically subjective, objective and possessive, in that order. That's why I can never be correct if I write or say, "This is him."

The key to understanding pronoun complements is an understanding of linking verbs. It's simple. Linking verbs are followed by nouns and pronouns that must be written in the subjective case form. Predicate nouns present no problems because, unlike pronouns, they are spelled the same in both the subjective and objective cases. If the noun *love* is the subject of the verb, it is spelled *love*. If the noun *love* is the direct object of the verb it is still spelled *love*. The noun *love* and all other nouns in English change form only in the possessive case. Pronouns are different from nouns, and pronoun spellings must be learned word by word, case by case. I must know that *he,* whenever written or spoken, is always the subjective case form. I must know that *him* is always the objective case form of this pronoun. I must know that *his* is always the possessive case form of this pronoun. If this rule gives you problems, just make up a few little sentences. Thinking of the love of God for me, I would never write or say, "*Him* loves me." Wrong! I need the subject case form because I am writing a pronoun subject (the subjective case form of the pronoun *he)* Therefore, "*He* loves me." And thinking of my love for God, I would never write or say, "I love *he.*" Wrong again. I need the objective form of the pronoun; I must say, "I love *him.*"

Some examples of pronouns in the subjective case (subjects of verbs) are *he*, *she*, *we* and *they*. Those same pronouns in the objective case are *him*, *her*, *us* and *them*. The possessive case spelling of those pronouns are *his*, *her/hers*, *our* and *theirs*.

Very few people on the streets of America know the grammatical difference between *This is he* and *This is him*. Understanding the complement clarifies the distinction between the two. And besides, our standard for learning the language does not come from the streets of America. Rather, we want our standard of correctness to flow into the streets of America.

Predicate Adjective Again

Now we want to spend a quiet moment with our old friend, the predicate adjective. Like the predicate noun it poses no problem because it does not change spelling as a predicate adjective from a regular adjective. The examples below following the verb are all predicate adjectives and receive the wavy line underneath when we decorate them because they are complements.

Just then Saul was returning from the fields . . . and he asked, "What is **wrong** with the people? Why are they weeping?" **(1 Sam. 11:5)**

Praise the LORD, for the LORD is **good**; sing praise to his name, for that is pleasant. (Psalm 135:3)

They risked their lives for me. Not only I but all the churches of the Gentiles are **grateful** to them. (Rom. 16:4)

What I mean, brothers, is that the time is **short.** (1 Cor. 7:29)

Dear friend, you are **faithful** in what you are doing for the brothers, even though they are strangers to you**.** (3 John 1:5)

The voice of the LORD is **powerful**; the voice of the LORD is **majestic**. **(Psalm 29:4)**

Whenever we decorate we write a wavy line beneath each of these predicate adjectives that we now know as complements. **Bold** type identifies the seven predicate adjectives in the examples just listed. Each could be written as a regular adjective describing the noun following it: a *wrong* what, a *good* Lord, *grateful* churches, *short* time, *faithful* you and *powerful* voice and *majestic* voice. Please note that the seven adjectives, *wrong*, *good*, *grateful*, *short*, *faithful*, *powerful*, and *majestic*, are spelled the same whether they are predicate adjectives or regular adjective modifiers.

To recap, the eight marks used to decorate sentences are two lines under the complete verb, one line under the subject, three lines under the direct object, four lines under an indirect object, a wavy line under complements, [brackets] around complete clauses and (parentheses) around phrases. The purpose of decorating sentences is to edit them. Step one of editing is to eliminate errors—subject-verb agreement errors, avoiding fragments, misplaced modifiers, pronoun reference problems, etc. Learning to decorate your sentences will take you along the road to clear, confident editing.

Review Questions for Chapter Seven: Decorating Sentences

1. How is decorating sentences different from diagramming them?
2. How many marks are used to decorate sentences?
3. Write all those marks and write beside them what each one indicates.
4. How do we decorate John 11:35, "Jesus wept"?
5. Is "Jesus wept" a clause, and if so, what kind? Explain.
6. What mark in decorating sentences indicates phrases?
7. What mark in decorating sentences indicates clauses?
8. What three steps are taken in what we call the clause test?
9. Name the two groups of words that change independent clauses to dependent clauses?
10. The acronym FANBOYS stands for what group of words? Name the seven words.
11. Do good writers begin sentences with coordinate conjunctions such as *and, but* and *so*?
12. Name four great writers who begin sentences with *and* and *but*.
13. Name the three verbals.
14. Explain the difference between a direct object and a complement.
15. A complement can be what three parts of speech?
16. What kinds of verbs have direct objects following them?
17. What kind of verbs have complements following them?
18. Define predicate.
19. A predicate noun renames what?
20. A predicate adjective describes what?

EIGHT

Verbs, Nouns' Best Friends

Professor Patricia T. O'Conner, in her indispensable *Woe Is I*, says of verbs that they keep nouns from "standing around with their hands in their pockets" (49). Of the power of verbs no one has said it better. Because writing cannot exist without verbs and because skillful use of verbs offers so much opportunity to support and strengthen writing, I devote this chapter to them. Verbs tell what nouns and pronouns are doing. Verbs are the most interesting words in the sentence, and they are multifaceted. Verbs have *jobs*, *tenses*, *names*, *voices* and *moods*.

VERBS HAVE JOBS

Verbs Show Action (Happenings) or State of Being

The clause is the heart of the sentence; the verb is the heart of the clause. If there is no verb, there is no clause; if there is no clause, there is no sentence. Since a verb is essential to every sentence, let us master exactly what the verb is and what it does. A verb possesses one of two talents, never both at the same time. Every verb has the job of showing an action, or it has the job of showing a state of being. No verb can show an action and a state of being at the same time. A verb exists in order to show an action, or it exists in order to show a state of being.

Action Verbs in Exodus 19:4 and Mark 3:13

It makes sense to look first at action verbs because strong writing depends on them. Exodus 19:4 in the New Living Translation reads:

> You have seen what I did to the Egyptians. You know how I brought you to myself and carried you on eagle's wings.

The two sentences in this verse contain five action verbs—*have seen, did, know, brought* and *carried*. Each verb shows a particular action taking place, something happening: *seeing, doing, knowing, carrying* and *bringing*.

Exodus 19:4 delivers a message of protection that brings "the peace of God that passes understanding" (Phil. 4:7). And the assurance of protection comes through the verbs. The people *see* through their eyes what God did to the Egyptians. The people *know* in their hearts how they *were carried* to safety. The power of being carried on eagle's wings is understood best when we know how the mother carries her young. She tucks them against her body as she soars; only the mother's death could make her relinquish her hold. Then, best of all, Yahweh says not only that he has carried Israel into safety but also that he has carried her unto himself. The object of Yahweh's love is the nation of Israel; the journey takes his people of Israel out of danger into safety and finally into the heart of God. As the loving mother eagle protects her babies, so the Lord cradles his people.

Think of the subject of an action verb as an actor on stage or screen. In Exodus 19:4 the subject of the verb is the word that names the doer of the action. The first subject-verb cluster in Exodus 19:4 is *You have seen.* The subject *you* is the actor on the stage, and the action is *have seen.* Note that the verb *seen*, from the infinitive *to see*, includes the auxiliary (helping) verb *have*. Complete verbs sometimes contain more than one word. We will cover that topic shortly.

The remaining verbs in this metaphor speak power. The subjects of the first and third verbs (*have seen* and *know*) are *you* respectively. The actor in the remaining three verbs is God, or since he is speaking of himself, *I, I did, I brought* and *I carried* conclude the five subject-verb clusters in this compound sentence. The poetry in this expression of protection and warmth makes us want to leave the grammar and bask in the comfort of the writing. However, our business here is grammar, and we cannot leave it for too long, so let us let the precision of the verbs reflect the power of the writing. Verbs carry the message. The writers of the Holy Scripture inspire us with verbs as they carry their messages of love. And Exodus 19:4 is a prime example of clear writing that uses action verbs, not state of being verbs. From this verse we discover how action verbs do their job: they work; they move; they carry the water; they move readers. God is both the active participant and the central character.

Mark 3:13 reads, "Jesus went up on a mountainside and called to him those he wanted, and they came to him." Note in this verse the four action verbs. The first three verbs show different acts performed by Jesus; the fourth verb shows a single act by the crowd. Remember that action verbs tell what is taking place, what is happening. This verse describes three of Jesus' actions: he *went,* (he) *called* and (he) *wanted*. In response to his three actions, "they came to him."

VERBS HAVE TENSES

Verb tense conveys time. Verbs show tense (time) by changing form. English has six verb tenses, divided into two groups: simple and perfect. The three simple tenses divide time into present, past and future. The present tense describes what happens regularly, what takes place in the present, or what is consistently or generally true. The past tense tells of an action completed or a condition ended. The future tense indicates action yet to be taken or a condition not yet experienced.

Present, Present Perfect, Past and Future Tense Verbs from Revelation 21:3-4.

> And I **heard** [past tense] a loud voice from the throne saying, "Now the dwelling of God **is** [present tense] with men, and he **will live** [future tense] with them. They **will be** [future tense] his people, and God himself **will be** [future tense] with them and [**will**] **be** [future tense] their God. He **will wipe** [future tense] every tear from their eyes. There **will be** [future tense] no more death or mourning or crying or pain, for the old order of things **has passed** [present perfect tense] away.

And as though these promises for the future were not enough, the one sitting on the throne tells John (Rev. 21:5b-7) to

> **Write** [present tense] this down, for these words **are** [present tense] trustworthy and true . . . It **is done** [present tense] I **am** [present tense] the Alpha and Omega, the Beginning and the End. To him who **is** [present tense] thirsty I **will give** [future tense] to drink without cost from the spring of the water of life. He who **overcomes** [present tense] **will inherit** [future tense] all this, and I **will be** [future tense] his God and he **will be** [future tense] my son.

Use the present tense to state a general truth:

> You **are** all sons of God through faith in Christ Jesus. (Gal. 3:26)

Use the past tense to show earlier action:

> In the beginning God **created** the heavens and the earth. (Gen. 1:1)

Use the future tense for action to come:

> I warn you, as I did before, that those who live like this **will** not **inherit** the kingdom of God. (Gal. 5:21b)

Note the tenses used in this last verse: *warn* (present), *did* (past), *live* (present), *will* (not) *inherit* (future).

The Present Perfect Tense (a Glimpse)

The three perfect tenses also divide time into present, past and future. They show more complex time relationships than the simple tenses. The three simple tenses and the three perfect tenses also have progressive forms. These forms indicate that whatever the verb describes is ongoing and continuing.

Christ has loved the church since the foundation of the world.

We are not tempted to say, "Christ has loven," or even "Christ has love the church." Our ears usually tell us the correct form because we have heard more often than not the correct form of the present perfect tense. The present perfect tense is formed every time by placing *has* or *have* in front of the past participle. If the subject is plural, the auxiliary (helping) verb is *have*, except for the first and second person singular (*I have* and *you have*). People *have followed* the teachings of Jesus since he walked the face of the earth. The verb *have followed* in the previous sentence is the present perfect tense as well as *Christ has loved* in the sentence above this paragraph.

Matthew 23:23 contains two present perfect tense verbs:

> Woe to you, teachers of the law and Pharisees, you hypocrites! You give a tenth of spices—mint, dill and cumin. But **you have** neglected the more important matters of the law—justice, mercy and faithfulness. **You should have practiced** the latter without neglecting the former.

Mark 6:2b contains one present perfect tense verbs:

> What's this wisdom **that has been** given him, that he even does miracles.

Make Flash Cards

We have not mentioned recently the need to make 3 × 5 flash cards. These cards are for memorizing. Write on the blank side of the card, "Present Perfect Tense." On the lined side of the card, remind yourself that this tense is formed by *have* or *has* written just before (in front of) the past participle. The past participle is the third principal part of the verb, as shown in our list later in this chapter. The present perfect tense comes clear to most of my students when they think of this tense as continued action that has taken place over a period of time in time past. For example,

I will not venture to speak of anything except what Christ **has accomplished** through me in leading the Gentiles to obey God by what I **have said** and **done**. (Rom. 15:18)

No bird of prey knows that hidden path, no falcon's eye **has seen** it. (Job 28:7)

The present perfect tense verbs above are formed by using the auxiliary verbs *has* or *have*. The three present perfect tense verbs from the two examples above are *has accomplished, have said, have done* and *has seen*. The message of the first sentence is Paul's stating that because of what Christ accomplished in the past and continues to accomplish in him, he (Paul) led and is still leading Gentiles to God by what Paul said and is continuing to say and do. That's continued action in time past. The second sentence uses the present perfect form of the verb *to see* in order to inform the reader that the bird did not see the path in the past and is continuing presently not to see the path. Subjects and verbs, as you know, must agree in number.

The Past Perfect Tense and Review of Present Perfect Tense

Hodges' Harbrace Handbook, fifteenth edition, states the following in explaining this tense: "The past perfect tense refers to an action completed at a time in the past prior to another past time or past action" (134). On the forming of the past perfect tense the same text says, "The past perfect tense is formed by combining the past tense of the auxiliary verb *had* with the past participle of the verb. There is only one form of the past perfect for regular verbs" (134). While *have* and *has* are indicators of the present perfect tense, *had* is the only indicator of the past perfect tense.

The past perfect tense of the verb stem *to see* down the page (vertical) not across the page (horizontal) as it is now. Also show Singular and Plural above the three persons:

| I **had** seen | You **had** *seen* | He, She It **had** *seen* |
| We **had** seen | You **had** *seen* | They **had** *seen* |

The past perfect tense of the verb stem *to do* read down the page, not across the page and show Singular and Plural above each:

| I **had** done | You **had** *done* | He, She, It **had** *done* |
| We **had** done | You **had** *done* | They **had** *done* |

An understanding of how to form these two tenses will prevent our saying, "I seen him when he done it." These verb stem infinitives, *to see* and *to do*, are both irregular verbs. The past tense and past participle forms of irregular verbs such as *to see* and *to do* are not the same. The past tense form of *to see* is *saw* while the past participle form is *seen*. The past tense never has an auxiliary (helping) verb before it while the past participle always has the auxiliary (helping) verb in front of it. Thus, "I *saw* him when he *did* it" is the correct past tense form, with its action completed in past time. But "I *seen* him when he *done* it" is incorrect because the sentence employs the past participle of an irregular verb, in each case, as the past tense form of the verb. Grammatically, this usage cannot stand.

Imagine for a moment an international student studying English for the first time. He hears no difference in the two expressions, *I saw him when he did it* and *I seen him when he done it*. In this situation, the difference has to be explained grammatically. Again, no regular past tense verb ever has a helping (auxiliary) verb.

| Jesus ***saw*** the multitudes. | Correct |
| Jesus ***had saw*** the multitudes. | Incorrect |

On the other hand, when the past participle of an irregular verb is spoken or written, an auxiliary (helping) verb precedes it. This rule explains the difference between the incorrect example above and the correct example below.

Correct present perfect tense:

Jesus **has seen** the multitudes.

Correct past perfect tense followed by the correct regular past tense:

But he **had spoken** with the disciples before he saw the multitudes.

The *Simon and Schuster Handbook for Writers* defines the present perfect tense as follows: "The tense indicating that an action or its effects, begun or perhaps completed in the past, continued into the present" (836). *Hodges' Harbrace Handbook*, fifteenth edition, commenting on the present perfect tense, states, "The Present Perfect Tense is formed by combining the helpers *have*, *has* (third person singular) with the past participle of the main verb" (133). *Hodges'* further explains that the past participle, the third principal part, remains the same regardless of person and number. But the auxiliary verbs used to form the present perfect tense have two forms, *have* and *has*. The key to recognizing and creating the present perfect tense is the auxiliary or helping verb. Either *have* or *has* will appear every time directly in front of the present perfect tense verb. The key to recognizing and creating the present perfect tense is the auxiliary or helping verb. Remember, the main verb in this present perfect tense is formed by the past participle following the auxiliary verb. For example, many Christians on Easter Sunday exclaim, "Christ **has risen**." The joyful response is, "He **has risen** indeed." Both these sentences are written in the present perfect tense.

Make a note of the following points of grammar. First, either auxiliary verb *have* or *has*, coupled with the past participle, forms the present perfect tense. Second, no irregular past participle written alone ever forms a verb. It is not a verb; it is a verbal. A verbal never functions as a verb. We will look at verbals in our next chapter. *Christ risen* is not a sentence and cannot be a sentence because the verbal *risen* is not a verb. The present participle form of the verb stem infinitive *to rise* is *rising*, and it can never be a verb when written by itself. *Sun rising, Jim rising, I rising*, the word *rising* in these three expressions is a verbal, not a verb.

Look please into the Hebrew Bible for a few present perfect tense verbs. Lamentations 2:7 contains three independent clauses; each one is written in the present perfect tense. These verbs show action that continues for a time in the past.

> The Lord **has rejected** his altar and [**has**] **abandoned** his sanctuary. He **has handed** over to the enemy the walls of her palaces; they **have raised** a shout in the house of the Lord as on the day of an appointed feast. (Lam. 2:7)

The signs of the present perfect tense *have* and *has* are used. The first two auxiliary verbs in the verse are *has*. The first two complete verbs are *has rejected* and *(has) abandoned* in the first clause. In the second clause *has handed* is the verb in the present perfect tense. The last clause in the verse uses *have*, the plural auxiliary, because the subject is the plural pronoun *they*. Check the subject-verb clusters in the three clauses of this seventh verse. Three independent clauses make this a compound sentence, a type of sentence frequently written by the poets of the Hebrew Bible. The first two subjects are *Lord* and *he* respectively. *Lord* is singular; *he* is singular; the subject *they* requires the plural *have* in order to be its auxiliary verb.

Rebecca Elliott in *Painless Grammar* writes the following sentence as an example of the present perfect tense: "I **have eaten** pizza many times" (24). Her sentence teaches that the present perfect tense expresses action that continues in past time. Elliott's very next sentence, showing an example of the past perfect tense, teaches how this particular tense relates to the past tense. Professor Elliott's sentence reads,

I **had eaten** pizza just before you arrived. (24)

The auxiliary or helping verb for the past perfect tense is *had*, every time.

	Singular	**Plural**
1st person:	I *had* eaten	We *had* eaten
2nd person:	You *had* eaten	You *had* eaten
3rd person:	He, She, It *had* eaten	They *had* eaten

The past perfect tense, like the present perfect tense, employs the third principal part of the verb. It builds this past perfect tense by placing the auxiliary verb *had* directly in front of the past participle. As noted above the auxiliary verb *had* is constant in all three persons—first, second, third person, singular and first, second, third person, plural. Elliott's "I **had eaten** pizza just before you arrived" is a perfect example that illustrates the relationship between the past perfect tense and the past tense.

The following sentence shows this relationship between the past perfect tense and the past tense: "Peter **had denied** Jesus three times before the rooster crowed." Confusion is avoided by knowing that the past perfect tense, announced by the auxiliary *had*, describes point action, Peter's denying that has taken place earlier in time than the past tense action, the rooster's crowing of the past tense. Note a similar relationship in Genesis 31:54.

> He offered a sacrifice there in the hill country and invited his relatives to a meal. After they had eaten, they spent the night there.

State of Being Verbs

Whenever I teach grammar classes or while I hold conferences with students, I refer to a verb as a word that shows an action or a state of being. I like to say that verbs, like people, possess talents. They have jobs to do. Verbs that are "state of being verbs" possess the talent to show that state. They do not possess the talent to show action. I want to zoom in a bit closer in order to focus momentarily on the verb *to be*. Looking at our list of principal parts in *Sacred Grammar* or in any other text, we find the following information about the verb *to be*:

Present Stem	**Past Tense**	**Past Participle**
is, am, are	was, were	been

The verb stem *to be* is the primary state of being verb. The family of *to be* verbs requires special attention. Although the various forms of the verb *to be* appear to be tricky, they are manageable. The forms of the verb *to be* in the present tense are the following: I *am*, you *are*, he, she, it *is*, we *are*, you *are*, they *are*. These six words are used to form the present tense of the verb *to be*; first, second and third person, singular and plural of the present tense.

	Singular	**Plural**
1st person:	I *am*	We *are*
2nd person:	You *are*	You *are*
3rd person:	He, She, It *is*	They *are*

The past tense forms of the verb *to be*, first, second and third person singular and plural are as follows:

	Singular	**Plural**
1st person:	I *was*	We *were*
2nd person:	You *were*	You *were*
3rd person:	He, She, It *was*	They *were*

Note please that thus far the present tense of this highly irregular verb has used the verbs I *am,* you *are,* he, she, it *is;* we *are,* you *are* and they *are*. The past tense has used the verbs I *was,* you *were,* he, she, it *was,* we *were,* you *were* and they *were*, respectively. The present tense and the past tense of the verb *to be* use only the first and second principal parts of the verb. This practice leaves only the third principal part of the verb, which is the past participle *been*. The perfect tenses (present, past and future) are formed only with an auxiliary verb before (in front of) the past participle *been*. The auxiliary verb's presence prevents any such nonsense such as, "I seen him when he done it." The three perfect tenses, the present perfect tense, the past perfect tense and the future perfect tense conjugate as follows:

The Present Perfect Tense of Being Verbs

	Singular	**Plural**
1st person:	I *have been*	We *have been*
2nd person	You *have been*	You *have been*
3rd person:	He, She, It *has been*	They *have been*

In the conjugation of the present perfect tense above, note that the auxiliary verbs *have* and *has* are the only signs or indicators of the present perfect tense. And *has*, not *have*, is used only in the third person singular form of the verb.

The Past Perfect Tense of Being Verbs

	Singular	**Plural**
1st person:	I *had been*	We *had been*
2nd person:	You *had been*	You *had been*
3rd person:	He, She, It *had been*	They *had been*

The auxiliary verb *had* is the only sign or indicator of the past perfect tense, as you can see in the above table. Very simply, all six persons, singular and plural, in the past perfect tense use *had* as the auxiliary verb.

The Future Perfect Tense of Being Verbs

	Singular	**Plural**
1st person:	I *will have been*	We *will have been*
2nd person:	You *will have been*	You *will have been*
3rd person:	He, She, It *will have been*	They *will have been*

The parsing of a verb determines five properties of its being: tense, mood, voice, person and number. The *tense* above is *future perfect*. The *mood* is *indicative*; something is happening, taking place. The *voice* is either *active* or *passive*, determined by whether the subject is acting or being acted upon. The voice of this verb is active. The person of a verb is determined by first, *I*; second, *you*; or third, *he, she* or *it*—singular. The plural options of the person are first, *we*; second, *you*; or third, *they*. The number of a verb is determined whether its subject is singular or plural (more than one).

More Specific Points about the Verb *To Be*

Grammar texts use various terms to describe certain aspects of the verb *to be*. We have looked briefly at the forms of this slippery verb in the present, past, present perfect, past perfect and future perfect tenses. Grammarians give this verb many names. We can simplify all this by learning that no form of the verb *to be* as a main verb will ever be followed by a direct object or any objective case form pronoun, such as *him*, *us* or *me*.

Examples from John's Gospel Using the Verb *To Be*

I want to go straight to four verses in John's Gospel that illustrate this "no objective case" after the verb *to be*. Learn this and stay clear on it, and you will never, ever again say, "This is her." You'll know why "This is she" is correct. For most of us, our ears won't help us know why "We are they" is correct, at least not until they are well trained on correct grammar.

Knowing a few specific points of grammar will help us. I love the fact that the following four examples are quotes from Jesus of Nazareth. Of course Jesus spoke Aramaic, but the English translations of the Greek are grammatically perfect as are the Aramaic words he spoke. Jesus spoke flawless grammar.

For the first example we go back to John 13:18, 19 where Jesus is predicting Judas's betrayal of him. Note that the adding of the apostrophe *s* (*'s*) is correct because the ear wants to hear a second *s* sound. No *s* after the apostrophe (') is needed for the singular possessive case of Moses' because the word already has two *s* sounds. John 13:18 quotes Psalm 41:9 when King David bemoans betrayal by a close associate. John 13:19 focuses on the closeness of the betrayer. Both David and Jesus paint the image of breaking bread together. John 13:19 reads,

> I am telling you now before it happens, so that when it does happen you will believe that I am He.

The last clause in the verse, *that I am he,* is dependent because it is introduced by the relative pronoun *that*. The main verb is *am*. The subject-verb cluster is *I am*. The one word following this particular form of the verb *to be* is the pronoun *he*. What is the case of the pronoun *he*? Of course, it's the subjective case; in class I like to call it the subject case because the subjective case is always the subject of the verb or it is a word related to or tied to the subject of the verb. The pronoun, *he*, here could not be *his* or *him* because neither the possessive case form nor the objective case form can correctly replace the subjective case. The correctly written *I am He* brings into play the rule that states that the verb *to be* or any form of it cannot be followed by the objective case. The verb is linking the subject to a word in the predicate that renames the subject of the verb. The renaming word is *he*. If you are ever tempted to say, "I am him" or "This is her" or "It is him" or "These are them" or "It is her," remember that the objective case of any pronoun following any form of the verb *to be* is incorrect. Each of these five little statements in the previous sentence is incorrect because each pronoun in the predicate is written as an object in the objective case. When written correctly they will read, "I am he" and "This is she" and "It is he" and "These are they" and "It is she." Each of these five pronouns in the predicate is written correctly in the subjective case form. They are called predicate complements. They rename their subjects. They are not direct objects; no form of the verb *to be* is ever followed by a word written in the objective case. Jesus said, "I am *he*," and his grammar is perfect.

Three additional verses in John's Gospel illustrate the point exactly: John 18:5, 6 and 8. The religious officials present, accompanied by Judas and soldiers, were seeking Jesus in order to crucify him. When Jesus asked members of the group whom they wanted, they replied, "Jesus of Nazareth." And Jesus said, "I am *he*." (And Judas the traitor was standing there with them.) Please note that Jesus does not say, "I am him." Jesus uses the word *he*, the subjective case form of the pronoun. In this statement *he* is joined to its subject *I* by the linking verb *was*.

The very next verse, John 18:6, makes the identical statement.

> When Jesus said, "I am *he*," they drew back and fell to the ground.

Incidentally, you want to be sure that you understand why "they drew back and fell to the ground." Consult a good commentary in order to unravel this puzzling passage. And again in verse eight Jesus said to the gathering crowd, including the chief priests and Pharisees, "I told you that I am *he*." The predicate of a sentence includes the complete verb plus all the remaining words that follow in its clause. The four words *that I am he* contain the main verb *am*. It is a popular, much used form of the verb *to be*. Therefore, the pronoun *he* that follows is written in the subjective case form. In each of the examples above, the verb, *am*, links its subject, *I*, to the predicate complement, *he*. The term predicate complement refers to a noun, pronoun or adjective that follows a linking, intransitive verb, which we will explain shortly. A predicate noun or pronoun renames the subject. A predicate adjective describes the subject. Nouns and pronouns that follow action, transitive verbs are called direct objects and receive the action of the verb.

| Correct: | I am *he*. |
| Incorrect: | I am him. |

Tense Sequences

Verb tense sequences show time relationships from one clause to another in a sentence. They help deliver messages about actions, occurrences, or conditions that take place at different times in the same sentence.

If an independent clause contains a simple present tense verb, then the dependent clause can use the present tense to show same-time action:

> A man **reaps** what he **sows**. (Gal. 6:7b)

He reaps *now* or always what he sows *now or always*.

Use the past tense in the dependent clause to portray action earlier than the action in the main clause:

> Now, brothers, I **know** that you **acted** in ignorance. (Acts 3:17a)

I know *now* that you acted in ignorance *before now, in the past*.

In the independent clause you can use the present perfect tense to show a period of time extending from some point in the past to the present (or) an indefinite past time:

> Those who belong to Christ Jesus **have crucified** the sinful nature with its passions and desires. (Gal. 5:24)

If an independent clause contains a past tense verb, then the dependent clause can use the past perfect tense to show earlier action:

> Jesus **knew** that the time **had come** for him to leave this world and go to the father. (John 13:1b)

If an independent clause contains a present perfect or past perfect tense verb, then the dependent clause following it can use the past tense:

He is not here; he has **risen**, just as he **said**. (Matt. 28:6a)

If your independent clause contains a future tense verb, then the dependent clause can use the present tense to show action happening at the same time:

> The Lord **will grant** that the enemies who **rise** up against you **will be defeated** before you. (Deut. 28:7)

Use the present perfect tense to show future action earlier than the action of the independent clause verb:

> Seven days from now I will **send** rain on the earth for forty days and forty nights, and I will wipe from the face of the earth every living creature I **have made**. (Gen. 7:4)

As you use the correct tense sequences, they will become automatic.

VERBS HAVE NAMES

At this juncture let us look at the different categories or names of verbs as they are described by most grammarians—*main* verbs, *linking* verbs, *auxiliary* and *modal auxiliary* verbs, *transitive* and *intransitive* verbs, and *regular* and *irregular* verbs.

Main Verbs

A verb expressing action, occurrence, or state of being that anchors an independent clause. The following examples come from verses in the NIV translation of both the Hebrew Bible and the New Testament unless noted otherwise.

John 18:12b	They **bound** him. (action)
John 18:14a	Caiaphas **was** the one. (state of being)
Exodus 22:3	But if it **happens** after sunrise, he is guilty of bloodshed. (occurrence)

Daniel 1:5a	The king **assigned** them a daily amount of food and wine from the king's table. (action)
Jeremiah 27:18a	If they **are** prophets and **have** the word of the Lord. *are* = (state of being); *have* = (action)
Job 32: 6	So Elihu son of Barakel said, "I **am** young in years, and you **are** old." *am* and *are* = (state of being verbs) Both of these verbs link the adjectives that follow them to their subjects, *I* and *you*. Both *young* and *old* modify the subjects, *I* and *you*, respectively.
Job 40:4a	I **am** unworthy. (state of being)

Linking Verbs

A linking verb is one that shows a state of being (*is*) or one that relates to the senses (*taste*) or one that indicates a condition (*grow*), and it always joins a subject to a word or words that rename or describe it.

> For they said, "The people have **become** hungry and tired and thirsty in the desert." (2 Sam. 17:29b)

> The linking verb *become* joins the adjective complements *hungry, tired, thirsty* to the subject *people* to report something about the *people*.

> She **is** pillaged, plundered, stripped! Hearts melt, knees give way, bodies tremble, every face **grows** pale. (Nah. 2:10)

> The linking verb *is* in the first sentence of the Nahum passage joins *she* to the adjective complements *pillaged, plundered, stripped*. In the second sentence the linking verb *grows* links *face* to the adjective that describes it, *pale*.

Auxiliary Verbs

An auxiliary verb is one that combines with a main verb to indicate tense, mood, or voice. Auxiliary verbs are also called helping verbs.

a. But I **have** stilled and **(have)** quieted my soul. (Psalm 131:2a) The auxiliary verb *have* forms the present perfect tense of *stilled* and *quieted*.
b. If only you **had** paid attention to my commands, your peace **would have** been like a river, your righteousness like the waves of the sea. (Isa. 48:18) (**had** paid attention = past perfect tense); (would **have** been = present perfect tense).
c. Because I **will** not listen. (Jer. 11:14b) = (future tense)

Modal Auxiliary Verbs

Modal pertains to mode, manner or form. Auxiliary verbs known as *modal* indicate capability, desire, necessity, permission, possibility. Modal auxiliary verbs are used with the base form of another verb to express distinctions of mood. Some modal auxiliary verbs include *can, could, may, might, ought, shall, should, will, would* and *must*. The modal auxiliary verb joins the main verb in order to indicate mood. The modal auxiliary verb *would* indicates the subjunctive mood in "I *would* be good if I could." The modal auxiliary *may* appears in Habakkuk 2:2: "Then the Lord replied: Write down the revelation and make it plain on tablets so that a herald may run with it."

Then the Lord replied:	**(past tense)**
Write down the revelation	(imperative mood)
and make it plain on tablets	(imperative mood)
so that a herald may run with it.	(subjunctive mood because of modal verb *may*)

"We **should** choose a leader and go back to Egypt" (Num. 14:4), subjunctive mood because of the modal verb *should*.

Transitive and Intransitive Verbs

Remember our discussion of transitive and intransitive verbs way back where we learned about direct objects, indirect objects and complements? Here we go again. A transitive verb is a verb that is followed by a direct object—a noun or a pronoun that completes the verb's message. The Latin word for transitive is *transitivus,* or passing over as from the subject to the object. The subject's action in a transitive verb's clause passes through the verb to the direct object: the transitive verb conveys that action from the subject over to the direct object. That is, in order to be transitive in a sentence, a verb must be followed by a (noun or pronoun) direct object. *Sacred Grammar* has cited John 11:35 many times. It reads, "Jesus wept." The verb *wept* from the verb stem *to weep* is listed in most dictionaries first as both a transitive and as an intransitive verb. This is correct because *Jesus wept* has no direct object while *Jesus wept tears* uses the transitive verb whose direct object is *tears.* Jonah 3:3a provides a transitive verb having a clear direct object.

Jonah **obeyed** the word of the Lord and went to Nineveh.

An *intransitive* verb, on the other hand, does not have a direct object in order to complete its message. A verb is intransitive when an object is not required to complete its meaning. Isaiah 12:5 says, "**Sing** to the Lord, for he has done glorious things." The intransitive verb *sing* is followed by a prepositional phrase, which modifies the verb. This phrase does not receive the action of the verb; therefore, it is not a direct object. The subject of *sing* is the understood *you*. The verb is intransitive complete and is in the imperative mood because it gives a command or an order or directive.

A verb is transitive when a direct object completes its meaning. And as you shall see, a word that stands as an intransitive complete verb in one verse might appear in another verse as transitive. Isaiah 23:16 says, "**Play** the harp well, **sing** many a song, so that you will be remembered." The direct object *harp* answers the question, what word receives the action of the verb? *Play the harp.* And in the next clause, the direct object *song* answers the question, what word receives the action of the verb?" *Sing the song.* Note that *sing* appeared in Isaiah 12:5 as intransitive complete, since it had no direct object. *Play* is another word that might serve as both transitive and intransitive, depending upon its use. See if you can use *play* as a transitive verb and then as an intransitive verb.

Comparison of Intransitive and Transitive Verbs

In the following simple sentence, the verbs *went* and *sat* are intransitive. They have no direct objects. They are simply modified by adverbs.

"Then she **went** off and **sat** down nearby" (Gen. 21:16). *Off* and *down* are not direct objects; they are modifiers.

Another example of an intransitive verb is,

> And he uttered his oracle: "The oracle of Balaam son of Beor, the oracle of one whose eye **sees** clearly. (Num. 24:3) Clearly is not a direct object; it is an adverb modifier. And another is,

> For men **will hear** of your great name. (1 Kings 8:42)
> *Of your great name* is not a direct object; it is a modifier.

In the following sentences the verbs are transitive (having direct objects) because they carry the action of the verb from the subject to another noun or pronoun:

> When Delilah saw that he had told her everything, she **sent** word to the rulers of the Philistines. (Judges 16:18)

Word is a direct object. "He **sends** you abundant showers" (Joel 2:23). *Showers* is a direct object. *You* is the indirect object.

If I were to look at the base form of each of these verbs in collegiate dictionaries, I would find what are called indicators. They appear as abbreviations, such as *tr.* or *v.* or *v.i.* or *v.t.* Some of them appear in the following sentences. The abbreviation *v.* indicates verb. The abbreviations *tr.* and *v.t.* indicate transitive verb. Get familiar with good dictionaries and their helps. Remember that dictionaries help by giving us the part of speech along with the pronunciation and the definition for each word listed.

Be sure to understand that a verb in order to be transitive in a sentence has to have a direct object present. The verb *to weep* is listed *v.*, *v.i.* and *v.t.* in *Webster's New Universal Unabridged Dictionary.* In the sentence *Jesus wept* the verb is intransitive. There is no direct object; the subject-verb cluster is complete with no words following. However, *Jesus wept bitter tears* displays the direct object *tears* and the transitive verb *wept*.

Regular and Irregular Verbs

Regular verbs are friendly because they do not jump up and bite us. They don't bite us unless we confuse and mix them with the irregular ones. For instance, the popular verb *to love* is regular all day long. Its principal parts are *love, loved, loved.* The first verb in John 3:16 is *loved.* No one, to my knowledge, has ever miswritten or misquoted "for God so loved the world." We speak and write correctly that regular past tense form of the verb.

The Third Person Singular *S* Form of Present Tense Verbs

I want to address the *s* form of the verb before looking at any others. I see and hear countless errors in this third person singular regular present tense form of the verb. The frequency of this blatant error has reached epidemic proportions in my hearing. Please learn the following chart:

SINGULAR		**PLURAL**	
Person		Person	
1st	I sing	1st	We sing
2nd	You sing	2nd	You sing
3rd	He, She, It *sings*	3rd	They sing

The last letter of the verb in the third person singular column is *s*. It is of utmost importance to know that every verb form in English in the third person singular, regular present tense form ends with the letter *s*. He *sings;* she *sings;* it *sings;* he *prays*; she *prays*; it *prays*. Every noun or pronoun subject in the third person singular, regular present tense will always be followed by a verb that ends with the letter *s*. This rule applies only in the present tense; in class I refer to the present tense as the regular present tense. There are other present tense forms such as the progressive present tense: he *is singing;* she *is singing*; it *is singing.* The *s* form where the letter *s* always appears occurs only in regular present tense verbs.

Subject-Verb Agreement Error in *S* Form Verbs

Psalm 55:16b reads, "And the Lord saves me." Psalm 55:17b says, "And he hears my voice." Psalm 55:18a claims, "He ransoms me unharmed from the battle waged against me." Psalm 55:20a asserts, "My companion attacks his friends; he violates his covenant." Literally hundreds of third person singular, regular present tense verbs appear in the Bible. In every instance the verb ends with the letter *s*. My students note regularly that I hammer home this grammatical fact ad infinitum. A few feel that I hammer home the *s* form ad nauseam. Perhaps I protest a bit much. However, I grow weary of speakers and students and folks who should know better than to go around saying and even writing, "She *sing* in the choir." "He *preach* like a house afire." "God *love* the little children of the world." "It *bless* me every time I read it." "The sea *meet* the shore at the foot of the mountain." "That man *serve* God faithfully." "My professor *attend* chapel every time the door *open*." "This subject-verb agreement error *drive* me crazy!" "Paul *send* Timothy ahead to greet the people." "She *see* the light." "He *come* to the garden alone." These eleven subject-verb agreement errors are all corrected by adding the letters *s* or *es*. "She sings in the choir." "He preaches like a house afire." So forth and so on. The previous eleven sentences contain subject-verb agreement errors. Every subject is singular, only one actor; there is not one plural subject, but every verb in each of these incorrectly written sentences is plural. There is one cardinal rule in grammar that will never change: the subject and verb must agree in number. If the subject is singular, the verb must be singular. No exceptions in the indicative mood. Note that adding the letter *s* to the verbs corrects the error in each of the twelve sentences. These atrocious errors I have seen and heard most of my days. I long for the day when, in America, no eye will read nor any ear hear such rubbish. We cry for the clear, soft relief of precision.

The Counting-to-Two Remedy

The ability to count to two will help any writer avoid the subject-verb agreement error in the third person singular, regular present tense form of the verb. How do we get help by counting to two? We get help by counting the number of subjects or by determining if the noun or pronoun subject of the verb names a plural subject. If either example exists, the verb must be plural in order to agree in number with its subject.

Note: The man **runs** away because he is a hired hand and **cares** nothing for the sheep. (John 10:13)

Never: The man run away because he is a hired hand and care nothing for the sheep.

This singular verb forms are **runs** and **cares.**

Note: They **rush** upon the city; they **run** along the wall. (Joel 2:9)

The plural subject requires the plural verb form.

Never: They rushes upon the city; they runs along the wall.

The plural subject requires the plural verb form, *run*.

We conclude this *s* ending, third person singular, regular present tense verb form discussion with a few more verses from scripture. In the verses below each subject is singular (one actor); each verb in its subject-verb cluster agrees in number with its subject. Therefore, both the subject and the verb are singular.

Now Elijah the Tishbite, from Tishbe in Gilead, said to Ahab, As the Lord **lives**, whom I serve, there will be neither dew nor rain in the next few years except at my word. (1 Kings 17:1)

This quote from Elijah the prophet to Ahab the king begins, "As the Lord lives." The subject is *Lord* and the verb is *lives*. Can you imagine this verse in the Bible reading, "As the Lord *live*."? Please! Can you? *Count to two.* And please note that the third person singular regular present tense comes into play here. *Lord* is the singular subject of the singular verb, *lives*. Please circle and mark and highlight the letter *s* at the end of the singular verb, *lives*. The letter *s* on the end of present tense verbs indicates that they are singular.

For this is what the Lord, the God of Israel **says**. (1 Kings 17:14a)

The two verbs in this quotation are *is* and *says*. The first of these two verbs, a form of the verb *to be*, ends with the letter *s*. The singular pronoun *this* is the subject of the verb *is*. The second present tense verb *says* has the singular subject *Lord*. Verbs end with the letter *s* whenever they are in the present tense third person singular form.

In 1 Kings 17:14, we discover yet another third person singular, regular present tense verb at the end of the verse.

> For this **is** what the Lord, the God of Israel, **says**: "The jar of flour will not be used up and the jug of oil will not run dry until the day the Lord **gives** rain on the land."

The following dependent clause ends the verse: until the Lord gives rain on the land. Surely, we are sufficiently convinced that this verb form ends every time with the letter *s*.

Always: The Lord *gives*.

Never: The Lord *give*.

Avoiding Errors Using *S* Form Verbs

In order to avoid the third person singular present tense errors that we've just discussed, remember the following: the third person singular refers to a singular noun or pronoun that is the subject of its verb. Below is a column of singular pronoun subjects.

SINGULAR
I
you
he, she, it (or any singular noun)

Irregular Verbs

Verbs, regular and irregular, have what grammar books call principal parts. Each verb has three principal parts. Every tense in English is formed by starting with the three principal parts of the verb. The following list is compiled from several leading texts. The verbs are listed in alphabetical order; all are common *irregular* verbs. They are irregular because neither the past tense word nor the past participle word is formed by adding *d* or *ed*.

The Principal Parts of Irregular Verbs

Base or Simple Form	Past Tense	Past Participle
arise	arose	arisen
awake	awoke *or* awaked	awaked *or* awoken
be (is, am, are)	was, were	been
bear	bore	borne, born
beat	beat	beaten
become	became	become
begin	began	begun
bend	bent	bent
bet	bet	bet
bid "to offer"	bid	bid
bid "to command"	bade	bidden

Base or Simple Form	Past Tense	Past Participle
bind	bound	bound
bite	bit	bitten or bit
blow	blew	blown
break	broke	broken
bring	brought	brought
build	built	built
burst	burst	burst
buy	bought	bought
cast	cast	cast
catch	caught	caught
choose	chose	chosen
cling	clung	clung
come	came	come
cost	cost	cost
creep	crept	crept
cut	cut	cut
deal	dealt	dealt

dig	dug	dug
dive	dived *or* dove	dived
do	did	done
draw	drew	drawn
drink	drank	drunk
drive	drove	driven
eat	ate	eaten
fall	fell	fallen
feed	fed	fed
feel	felt	felt
fight	fought	fought
find	found	found
flee	fled	fled
fling	flung	flung
fly	flew	flown
forbid	forbade *or* forbad	forbidden
forget	forgot	forgotten
forgive	forgave	forgiven
forsake	forsook	forsaken
freeze	froze	frozen
get	got	got or gotten
give	gave	given
go	went	gone
grow	grew	grown
hang (to suspend)	hung	hung
hang (to execute)	hanged	hanged
have	had	had
hear	heard	heard
hide	hid	hidden
hit	hit	hit
hurt	hurt	hurt
keep	kept	kept

know	knew	known
lay	laid	laid
lead	led	led
leave	left	left
lend	lent	lent
let	let	let
lie	lay	lain
lie (to bear false witness)	lied	lied
light	lighted *or* lit	lighted *or* lit
lose	lost	lost
make	made	made
mean	meant	meant
pay	paid	paid
prove	proved	proved *or* proven
quit	quit	quit
read	read	read
rid	rid	rid
ride	rode	ridden
ring	rang	rung
rise	rose	risen
run	ran	run
say	said	said
see	saw	seen
seek	sought	sought
send	sent	sent
set	set	set
shake	shook	shaken
shine (to glow)	shone	shone
shine (to polish)	shined	shined
shoot	shot	shot
show	showed	shown *or* showed
shrink	shrank	shrunk

sing	sang	sung
sink	sank *or* sunk	sunk
sit	sat	sat
slay	slew	slain
sleep	slept	slept
sling	slung	slung
speak	spoke	spoken
spend	spent	spent
spin	spun	spun
spring	sprang *or* sprung	sprung
stand	stood	stood
steal	stole	stolen
sting	stung	stung
stink	stank *or* stunk	stunk
stride	strode	stridden
strike	struck	struck
strive	strove	striven
swear	swore	sworn
sweep	swept	swept
swim	swam	swum
swing	swung	swung
take	took	taken
teach	taught	taught
tear	tore	torn
tell	told	told
think	thought	thought
throw	threw	thrown
understand	understood	understood
wake	woke *or* waked	waked *or* woken
wear	wore	worn
wring	wrung	wrung
write	wrote	written

"I seen him when he done it."

The idea of regular and irregular verbs strikes fear in the hearts of many of us. We have said that verbs are slippery. They are, but the irregular fellows can be overcome by mastering just a few rules. Recently on prime-time American television, I heard a news-show guest say, "If he had wanted to be president, he *would have ran* more than once." Standing in line in my bank in a great Southern American city, I heard a homeowner speak this sentence into her cell phone: "My contractor *has did* a marvelous job remodeling my kitchen." The speaker on the television news show was explaining that a defeated candidate, in his opinion, could gain his party's support in the future. The person speaking of her kitchen showed satisfaction in the work completed. Most of the readers of this text cringe at *could have ran* in the television sentence as well as the *has did* sentence I heard in the bank. We cannot rely always on our ears. We want to have grammatical backup whenever we strive for correctness. Other than the stridency in our ears, what's wrong with *would have ran* and *has did*? Please don't forget my mythical cousins back in the mountains who say, "I seen him when he done it." Let me say it again. My "cousins" and others who butcher the language are not to be judged for their grammar. Surely, as bootleggers and preachers, sometimes at the same time, they are light-years ahead of me economically and spiritually. But they are not interested in correctness in spoken or written English. You and I are.

VERBS HAVE MOODS

The mood of a verb in a sentence shows the attitude toward the action. The concept of *mood* escapes some of my students until I talk with them about the study of poetry. One of the elements of any particular poem is its tone. The meaning of tone becomes clear when we think of attitude. Even the untrained ear can distinguish the different tones of a person's voice, whether the person shows anger or sadness, joy or doubt. The tones of a guitar or any other musical instrument differ markedly between the key of C and the key of A minor. The key of C is happy, light; the key of A minor is sad, somber. Thomas Hardy's poem "Neutral Tones," like its title, captures a bleak mood. Two people, once happy together, feel only coldness for each other. The tone is one of despair. The attitude is gloom. On the other hand, Gerard Manly Hopkins' poem "The Windhover" brings a tone of peaceful protection, an attitude of peace. Hopkins' bird hovers unmoved in a fierce wind. Hopkins names Christ as mankind's windhover who holds steady against every storm of life. The reader feels the difference in the two moods of these two settings. Knowing the differences enables the reader to understand the three moods of verbs in English: the *indicative* mood, the *imperative* mood and the *subjunctive* mood.

Indicative Mood

The indicative mood makes statements about real things, highly likely things, and asks questions about fact. Please understand that this mood is nothing exotic or hard to understand; of all verbs written, the overwhelming majority falls into the category of the indicative mood. Indicative verbs affirm, deny or inquire.

Examples of the indicative mood:

> The harvest is past; the summer is ended, and we are not saved. (Jer. 8:20) (real)

> The chief priests and the whole Sanhedrin were looking for evidence against Jesus so that they could put him to death, but they could not find any. (Mark 14:1b)

were looking = highly likely
could (not) find = real

> Simon, are you asleep? (Mark 14:37) (questioning about a fact)

> But Jesus remained silent and gave no answer. (Mark 14:61) (stating a fact)

Imperative Mood

The imperative mood makes demands and direct requests. Often the subject is omitted in an imperative sentence; nevertheless, the subject is assumed to be either *you* or one of the indefinite pronouns such as *anybody*, *somebody* or *everybody*.

> **Watch** out for teachers of the law. (Mark 13:38a) (*You*, understood, is the subject of the verb.)
>
> **Give** to Caesar what is Caesar's and to God what is God's. (Mark 12:17a) (*You*, understood, is the subject.)

Note that the verbs in both the indicative and imperative moods undergo no change in their forms. These two moods show an attitude toward the action of a verb in a sentence. We are not called upon to learn any change in the form of a verb in either the indicative or imperative moods. We must learn the attitudes that they convey in order to distinguish them from the third and last mood, the subjunctive mood. Among other things the indicative mood makes a statement; among other things the imperative mood gives a command. There are other factors in these two moods, but making a statement for the indicative mood and giving a command for the imperative mood provides a foundation from which to proceed.

Subjunctive Mood

The *subjunctive* mood is the most complicated of the three moods in English. A verb in the subjunctive mood indicates speculation, other unreal conditions, conjectures, wishes, recommendations, indirect requests or demands.

Some of the subordinate conjunctions that often signal the subjunctive mood are *if, as if, as though*, and *unless*.

> For the LORD had said to Moses, "Tell the Israelites, 'You are a stiff-necked people. If **I were** to go with you even for a

> moment, I might destroy you. Now take off your ornaments and I will decide what to do with you.'" (Exod. 33:5)

The subject-verb cluster *I were* is contrary to fact, written in the subjunctive mood. The Lord is not going with Israel; therefore, the plural form of the verb *were* is correct.

Grammar texts teach that the subjunctive mood is employed often in dependent clauses. Many times in *Sacred Grammar* subordinate conjunctions and relative pronouns are cited as words or groups of words that make clauses dependent. Often dependent clauses introduced by *if*, as in Exodus 33:5 above, introduce the subjunctive mood.

> Even though my illness was a trial to you, you did not treat me with contempt or scorn. Instead, you welcomed me as **if I were** an angel of God, as **if I were** Christ Jesus himself. (Gal. 4:14)

Paul the Apostle is neither *an angel of God* nor *Christ Jesus himself*. Both verbs that close this quotation are written in the subjunctive mood because both are contrary to fact statements. In the dependent clause the subjunctive mood signals that what the clause says is highly unlikely or simply not the case in reality.

The second category for using the subjunctive mood occurs in *that* (relative pronoun) clauses expressing wishes, indirect requests, demands or recommendations.

In the verses immediately preceding the following verse, Jesus has explained that the true disciple will never have any peace in this world's system. He is expressing here his awareness that the fire he comes to bring is not yet reality.

> I have come to bring fire on the earth, and how I wish it were already kindled! (Luke 12:49)

Modal auxiliary verbs *would, could, might* and *should* can convey speculations and conditions contrary to fact. For example, "But if the animals **were** weak, he **would** not place them there" (Gen. 30:42). *Would* is a modal auxiliary verb.

VERBS HAVE VOICE

The subject of a verb in every clause is the word that names the doer of the action or the subject of the state of being verb. Every subject is a noun or a pronoun. The voice of a verb determines whether the subject is acting or receiving the action of the verb. There are many more active voice verbs than passive voice. The passive voice should be used sparingly and only in specific instances.

> You aren't swayed by men, because you pay no attention to who they are. Tell us, then, what is your opinion? Is it right to pay taxes to Caesar or not? (Matt. 22:16b, 17)

Here the emphasis is on the subject *you*, and the speaker is Jesus, and he is being questioned and "set up" by the Pharisees' disciples. The point of the passage is that Jesus is being acted upon, or in this case *not* being acted upon. Jesus is *not* swayed. The point is that he is not doing the action, but the attempt is to act on him. Thus the writer uses the passive voice of the verb *to sway*, which emphasizes the receiver of the action or the receiver, or here of the nonaction. For example,

> passive voice: To all in Rome who **are loved** by God and called to be saints: Grace and peace to you from God our Father and from the Lord Jesus Christ. (Rom. 1:7)
>
> active voice: To all in Rome whom God **loved** and **called** to be saints: Grace to you and peace to you from God our Father and from the Lord Jesus Christ.

Good writers, teachers of writing and grammar texts discourage a heavy use of the passive voice where the subject is acted upon. However, the passive voice when the subject is acted upon is permitted, even encouraged, in specific instances. The first instance of this practice occurs whenever the doer of the action is unknown or unimportant. For example,

> The goat became very great, but at the height of his power his large horn **was broken** off. (Dan. 8:8) (Who or what broke the horn is unknown.)

At that time Moses **was born**, and he was no ordinary child. (Acts 7:20)

Another time that the passive voice works effectively occurs when the focus is on the action and not on the doer of the action. "Sometimes the action in the sentence is more important than the doer of the action. For example, if you want to focus on historical discoveries in the narrative, use the passive voice. Conversely, if you want to emphasize the people making the discoveries, use the active voice" (*Simon & Schuster*, 206).

Example of the active voice:

But the king of Assyria **discovered** that Hoshea was a traitor. (2 Kings 17:4)

Example of the passive voice:

Hoshea was discovered to be a traitor.

Example of active voice:

Even if these three men—Noah, Daniel and Job—were in it, they **could save** only themselves by their righteousness, declares the Sovereign LORD. (Ezekiel 14:14)

Example of passive voice:

Noah, Daniel and Job **could be saved** only by their righteousness.

The Publication Manual of the American Psychological Association (PMAPA) states, "Verbs are vigorous, direct commentators. Use the active rather than the passive voice" (Washington, PMAPA, 1964, 32). A reading of 1, 2 and 3 John from the New Testament shows that only a few verbs need to be written in the passive voice. Of the 132 verses in these seven chapters, only three contain passive voice verbs. The most effective way to avoid using the passive voice excessively is to write it only when it is necessary. And that is accomplished by following rules listed in this chapter. Note the passive voice verbs in the three epistles mentioned.

> In this way, **love is made** complete among us so that we will have confidence in the day of judgment. (1 John 4:17a)

In this verse the *love* is not doing the making. It is made; it is acted upon.

> But that you **may be rewarded** fully. (2 John 1:8b)

Here the one *to be rewarded* is being acted upon, not doing the acting. By using the passive voice the writer emphasizes that the reward comes through grace—unmerited favor not earned, perhaps not deserved. And the one receiving the reward has done nothing in order to receive it.

From the fourth Gospel, John 1:3, a passive voice verb appears early. John 1:3a reads,

> Through him all things **were made**.

Clearly the passive voice is preferred here because the emphasis lies not in the fact that something was made but in the one who did the making. We yearn now to launch into the world of verbs, writing with vigorous, strong choices in the active voice. However, we also remember a few exceptions where the passive voice needs to be implemented.

Study Questions for Chapter Eight: Verbs, Nouns' Best Friends

1. What does Patricia O'Conner say that verbs do for nouns?
2. Verbs possess two talents; name them.
3. Name and define the eight parts of speech. Be sure to write them on flash cards as they appear in the Parts of Speech Chart.
4. Define a clause.
5. When a verb is transitive, what follows it?
6. Where do we look first to find the part of speech of a particular word?
7. What is the antecedent of a pronoun?
8. A pronoun must agree in number with its antecedent. Here *number* means what?
9. Some grammar texts name a fourth principal part of the verb. Name that fourth principal part.

10. The *s* form appears in what tense, what person and what number of the verb?
11. What, according to Patricia O'Conner, is one cardinal grammar rule that will remain?
12. If a verb has a direct object, what do we name that verb?
13. There are two broad categories of verbs. One category is the action verb. The second is what?
14. The subject of a verb must be one of two parts of speech. Name the two.
15. What is the function of the subject of an action verb?
16. What is the function of the subject of a state of being verb?
17. A direct object answers what question?
18. Only nouns and pronouns serve as subjects of verbs. Every pronoun in written English must have what?
19. Write the pronoun that can refer to one person (singular) or to many people (plural)?
20. Verbs originate from their stems or roots. This is often called the infinitive. What are the second and third principal parts of the four verb stems in Exodus 19:4 to go, to call, to want, to come?
21. What is the figure of speech, metaphor or simile, found in Exodus 19:4?
22. Some grammar texts refer to only three principal parts of the verb. What does this text, *Sacred Grammar*, name the three columns?
23. What makes a verb a regular verb?
24. What makes a verb an irregular verb?
25. Which verbs in which tense in English always end with the letter—s?
26. Number 11 in this quiz asks a question that I want to ask again. What one cardinal rule of grammar will never change?
27. What is a compound subject?
28. Name the verb, its subject, the tense of the verb, the person of the noun subject, the number of the noun subject and the number of the verb in the following dependent clause taken from 1 Kings 17:1a: "As the Lord lives."
29. What is the error in the following sentence: "She sing in the choir."
30. What are the second and third principal parts of the verb stem (infinitive) *to lie*, meaning to rest or recline?

31. What are the second and third principal parts of the verb stem (infinitive) *to lie*, meaning to falsify, to bear false witness?
32. What are the second and third principal parts of the verb stem (infinitive) *to lay*, meaning to put or to place?
33. What are the second and third principal parts of the verb stem (infinitive) *to shine*, meaning to glow, to radiate?
34. What are the second and third principal parts of the verb stem (infinitive) *to shine*, meaning to polish?
35. What are the second and third principal parts of the verb stem (infinitive) *to shrink*?
36. Why is the verb *to do* (principal parts: do, did, done) an irregular verb?
37. Why is the verb *to see* (principal parts: see, saw, seen) an irregular verb?
38. Why is the verb *to love* (principal parts: love, loved, loved) a regular verb?
39. Why is the verb *to set* (principal parts: set, set, set) an irregular verb?
40. Name the helping (auxiliary) verbs for the present perfect tense.
41. Name the helping verb for the past perfect tense.
42. What verb tense is formed using the second principal part?
43. What verb tenses are formed using the third principal part?
44. Describe the time being described when using the present perfect tense.
45. Describe the time being described when using the past perfect tense.
46. Define a preposition.
47. Name the three cases in English.
48. What two parts of speech have case?
49. Every noun written in English in the possessive case contains what mark of punctuation?
50. Explain the case error in the following sentence: I am him.
51. Explain why "I am he" is correct.
52. Isaiah 49:16a (New Living Translation) reads, "See, I have written your name on my hand." What is the tense of the verb in that sentence from Isaiah?
53. What tense is indicated by the auxiliary helping verbs *have* and *has*?
54. Tense conveys what?

55. What is the function of a modal auxiliary verb?
56. Name the three perfect tenses.
57. Name the tenses in the following sentence: Dr. Chang *will have delivered* five thousand babies by the times she *has retired*.
58. Define mood.
59. Name the three moods in English.
60. Which of the three moods often omits using a subject of the verb?
61. The verb form does not change in what two moods?
62. List some words or groups of words that indicate the verb to follow is in the subjunctive mood.
63. A verb written in the indicative mood generally does what?
64. A verb written in the imperative mood generally does what?
65. Most verbs (the overwhelming majority) are written in what mood?
66. The voice of a verb determines what about its subject?
67. Name the two voices of verbs in English.
68. Which of the two voices is to be used sparingly?
69. First John 4:17a employs the passive voice: "In this way, love *is made* complete among us so that we will have confidence in the day of judgment." Explain the passive voice.
70. Name the traditional six tenses in English.

NINE

A Moment with Verbals

Recently I read Akhil Reed Amar's *America's Constitution: A Biography*. In the preface Amar regrets that most Americans are not acquainted with the eight-thousand-word document that we know as the Constitution of the United States. If I may draw a distant parallel, I regret that few of us who use and enjoy the English language know much of the grammar on which it is based. I speak of verbals to my college students and some of them think I have mispronounced the word *verbs*. My computer underlines in red every time I type the word *verbals*. Grammatical terms do not rank in the list of terms that pique our interests. Nonetheless, I want every reader of *Sacred Grammar* to become familiar with verbals. I like to call verbals the first cousins of verbs. We have taken a long look at verbs. Readers of *Sacred Grammar* who understand verbals will add ammunition to their arsenal of writing. They work for us. They come from verbs. To the unknowing, verbals look like verbs. They sound like verbs. Sometimes, they even parade as verbs. But they are not verbs.

We frequently use verbals, perhaps not knowing what we've done. But I want you to use them confidently because verbals, like complex sentences, make available to the writer a pinch of seasoning. The English language uses three verbals that pop-up in good writing. Although a verbal cannot do the work of a verb, the three verbals that can flavor writing are called gerunds, participles and infinitives. Verbals get their life source from verbs. Every verbal hides within itself the *verb stem*. Referring to our list of principal parts of verbs, we start with the simple form called the *verb stem*. A dozen verb stems come to mind; they are all *infinitives*: *to answer, to be, to become, to call, to devour, to enlist, to fabricate, to guess, to haul, to justify, to listen, to nourish, to repeat.* Dozens of infinitives could be added to this impromptu list of thirteen. From the simple or present tense form (the first principal part), we write the regular present tense, the present progressive tense and the future tense of a verb. From this simple form we also can build and write the three types of verbals: gerunds, participles and infinitives.

> Examples: Present tense verb: We *believe* his report.
> Present progressive tense: We *are believing* his report.
> Future tense: We *will believe* his report.
> Gerund: *Believing* is obeying.
> Participle: The *believing* church is the obeying church.
> Infinitive: *To believe* is to obey

Gerunds for Fun

Of the three verbals let us enjoy first the gerund. If a word is a gerund, it will always be used as a noun in its sentence. So every gerund functions in one of the ways that a noun functions. Nouns are words that name persons, places and things. They function as subjects of sentences; they function as objects of verbs. They function as objects of prepositions; they function as complements. A gerund is a verbal that always functions as a noun in the phrase or clause where it appears. Every gerund ends with *ing*.

One grammar rule requires that a noun or pronoun written in front of a gerund must be written in the possessive case form, possessive case before a gerund. Please say that rule again, aloud. A noun or pronoun written in front of a gerund must be written in the possessive case form.

> Example: His *leaving* made us sad. Correct

The noun subject *leaving* is a gerund that has been built on the simple form *to leave*. The pronoun immediately in front of the gerund must be written in the possessive case form.

> Example: *He leaving* made us sad. Incorrect
> Example: *Him leaving* made us sad. Incorrect

Each of the pronouns in the two immediate examples is incorrect because their cases are subjective and objective, respectively. The rule requires that a noun or pronoun before (in front of) a gerund must be written in the possessive case. Knowing why "*His leaving* made us sad" is correct is one of those little nuggets of knowledge that positively influences good writing. The underlying reason for the "possessive case before a gerund rule" is the need for the *presence* of an adjective in front of the gerund, in our example *leaving*. Only the possessive case form of a noun or a pronoun could serve as an adjective. The pronoun subjective form *he* cannot modify. The pronoun objective form *him* cannot modify. Only *His leaving* works.

Gerunds in the Bible

> It is Jesus' name and the faith that comes through him that has given complete **healing** to him, as you can all see. (Acts 3:16b)

In this verse the word *healing* is a verbal because it comes from or is built on the stem *to heal*. It is the direct object of the verb *has given*; only nouns or pronouns can be direct objects. The gerund *healing* ends with the letters *ing*. The gerund here is surely the noun object, and it gives a different flavor than that given by the regular noun. In the same chapter of Acts, the writer uses a gerund as the object of a preposition.

> Repent, then, and turn to God, so that your sins may be wiped out, that times of **refreshing** may come from the Lord. (Acts 3:19)

The gerund *refreshing* comes from the stem *to refresh*, and it is the object of the preposition *of*. Note how gerunds as objects in both these verses above broaden our choices of nouns. Creating a gerund, whether it is a noun subject or a noun direct object or an object of a preposition, expands the noun vocabulary of the writer. Gerunds can be found throughout the Bible. I want to say again that I don't want to turn your Bible study into a grammar lesson, but I want the reading of scripture to improve your writing skills. Most good writers improve by imitating other good writers. Generations have learned to read by reading the Bible. May this generation learn to write by reading the Bible.

Leviticus 7:16 reads,

> If, however, his **offering** is the result of a vow or is a freewill **offering**, the sacrifice may be eaten on the day he offers it, but anything left over may be eaten on the next day.

The word *offering* in the first instance in this verse is a gerund subject of the verb *is*. In the second *offering* is the predicate noun (complement) of the second verb, *is*. Notice that both gerunds are nouns; the first is a subject and the second is a predicate noun, renaming the subject.

> Serve the Lord with fear and rejoice with **trembling**. (Psalm 2:11)

Again, the gerund is the noun object of a preposition and comes from the verb stem *to tremble*. The characteristic—*ing* ending is consistent with all other gerunds.

> Because of the oppression of the weak and (because of) the **groaning** of the needy, I will now arise says the Lord. I will protect them from those who malign them. (Psalm 12:5)

The gerund *groaning* functions as the noun object of the preposition *of*.

In the following verse, Psalm 31:10, three prepositions have noun objects. A preposition as we have learned is a word that joins its object (noun or pronoun) to the rest of the sentence. Two of the prepositional phrases end with nouns that are not gerunds; one of the three objects of the preposition in this verse is, in fact, a gerund. Let's look.

> My life is consumed **by anguish** and my years **by groaning**; my strength fails because **of my affliction**, and my bones grow weak. (Psalm 31:10)

The three prepositional phrases are *by anguish* and *by groaning* and *of my affliction*. Which one uses a gerund as its noun object? The *by groaning* prepositional phrase is the one of the three that comes out of a verb stem *to groan*. The three principal parts of this regular verb are *groan, groaned, groaned*. It is a regular verb because the second and third principal parts are formed by adding a *d* or an *ed*. Get into the habit of stating the three principal parts of all verbs. If unsure check *Sacred Grammar* or any other good grammar text. They all include the alphabetized rows of principal parts: present stem, past tense, past participle. Gerunds expand our noun choices. Start right away expanding your writing boundaries by using gerunds. If writers of the Bible use gerunds, so can you.

Participles

Like the other two verbals the participle is not a verb but it comes out of or from a verb. Unlike the gerund the participle has no set ending on each word. And whereas gerunds always act as nouns, every participle functions as either an adjective or an adverb. Participles add to our adjective and adverb vocabulary each time they are created. The third principal part of irregular as well as regular verbs often forms effective participles. The present tense form of the verb is made into a participle by adding *ing*. If it modifies a noun or a pronoun, that new creation is a participle, acting as an adjective. If that participle modifies a verb, the new creation is an adverb. The same *ing* word can be a gerund if it functions as a noun. Remember that a word that is not a verb but comes out of a verb and modifies a noun, pronoun or verb is a participle. Before we look into the Bible, let's explain a few participles. Suppose we use the word *faithful* to modify a noun such as *disciple:*

Example: Andrew proved to be a faithful disciple.

The dictionary tells us that the word *faithful* is an adjective. If we change the word *faithful* to *believing,* the word describing the noun *disciple* is still an adjective, but it's an adjective with a twist. It's a participle because we can trace its source to a verb stem *to believe*. We cannot do that with the word *faithful*. No one has ever thought of a verb stem *to faith*. Any list of verb stems gives us potential participles.

While participles act most frequently as adjectives, they also have the capacity to act as adverbs to modify verbs. Examine the following sentence given in the third edition of *The Brief English Handbook* as an example of a participle modifying a verb (460): "He ran *screaming* down the street."

The italicized *screaming* is the participle modifying the verb *ran*. Here are a couple of examples from the Bible using participles as adverbs:

> A Canaanite woman from that vicinity came to him, **crying** out, "Lord, Son of David, have mercy on me!" (Matt. 15:22)

> While each man held his position around the camp, all the Midianites ran, **crying** out as they fled. (Judg. 7:21)

And now we look again at a participle used as an adjective.

> To the Israelites the glory of the Lord looked like a **consuming** fire on top of the mountain. (Exod. 24:17)

The writer of this verse has used a participle as an adjective to describe the noun *fire*. The source of this participle is the present stem *to consume*. The participle is the present progressive tense form *consuming*. Many regular adjectives could have been used to modify the noun *fire*; however, the writer has chosen instead the action-packed participle *consuming*.

> I will send wasting famine against them, **consuming** pestilence and deadly plague; I will send against them the fangs of wild beasts, the venom of vipers that glide in the dust. (Deut. 32:24)

Three modifiers grace this verse. All three appear in the first independent clause. All three are adjectives. The first two, *wasting* and *consuming*, came out of the verb stems *to waste* and *to consume*. The third modifier, *deadly*, is not a participle; it's a regular adjective, as with the faithful disciple cited earlier.

Somewhere along the way a good teacher told me to recognize many adverbs by their last two letters, *ly*. *Deadly*, in the verse above, ends with *ly*; however, it's an adjective because it modifies the noun *plague*. The *ly* does not make every word an adverb; in fact, *deadly* is an adjective because it modifies a noun, in this case the noun *plague*. It is true that many adverbs end with the letters *ly*. The part of speech of a modifier, however, whether adjective or adverb, is determined by the word that it describes. Adjectives modify only nouns and pronouns. Adverbs modify verbs, adjectives and other adverbs. All participles are modifiers; as adjectives they modify nouns and pronouns. As adverbs they modify verbs, adjectives and other adverbs.

Looking around the Bible we find participles everywhere in both the Hebrew Bible and the New Testament. Good writers write participles. Reading the Hebrew prophets is one of my treasured pleasures. Jeremiah is my favorite of the Hebrew prophets while Isaiah and several others run a close second. In my reading I note that the first verse in the book of Isaiah contains the word *concerning*, which looks very much like a participle. Let's move closer.

The fragment heading of Isaiah 1:1a in the NIV reads,

> The vision **concerning** Judah and Jerusalem that Isaiah son of Amoz saw during the reigns of Uzziah, Jotham, Ahaz and Hezekiah, kings of Judah.

The word *concerning* invites scrutiny, and it is an example of a word's functioning in several different ways, thus determining its part of speech in a sentence. Believe it or not the word *concerning* in this translation of this heading to the entire book is a preposition, a word that joins its object to the rest of the sentence. Here the four words *concerning Judah and Jerusalem* form a tidy little prepositional phrase that is sandwiched between the words *vision* and *that*. Prepositional phrases, like many other phrases, serve as modifiers, functioning as adjectives or as adverbs. The noun *vision* is described by the prepositional phrase *concerning Judah and Jerusalem*. We will look now at a few participles in the early chapters of Isaiah. You might, for fun, read a few chapters in Isaiah to see if you detect any participles. Be sure to use the NIV translation. Remember that a participle is a verbal that functions as either an adjective or an adverb. Make a note of what you find in, say, the first two chapters.

Our search for participles proves fruitful early in chapter 1. Isaiah 1:4a, like Isaiah 1:1a, is not a sentence but a fragment. It reads,

> Ah, sinful nation, a people loaded with guilt, a brood of evildoers, children given to corruption.

It repeats the pattern of the first verse in this chapter. The participles are *loaded* and *given*; like prepositions, these participles introduce phrases. A participle can function as either an adjective or as an adverb. Both *loaded with guilt* and *given to corruption* are participial phrases modifying the nouns, people and children, respectively. I can hear my students ask, "Why, Dr. Beaty, do you want us to know participles?" Here's why. Suppose the writer of verse four had written merely *a guilty people* and *corrupt children*, rather than *a people loaded with guilt* and *children given to corruption*. Which writing is more colorful? Which is stronger? Which better tells the story? Which better carries the water? We will improve our writing by imitating the writers of the Bible. Good writers often imitate other good writers.

Isaiah 1:5 shifts the tone of this diatribe directed at the nation of Judah. After asking two questions that indicate a sympathetic accuser, the writer describes the head and the heart with two participles.

Isaiah 1:5b reads,

> Your whole head is injured; your whole heart afflicted.

If we were decorating these two independent clauses, we would write two lines under the verb in the first clause. The second clause contains no verb; however, its verb is the understood verb *is* of the first clause. The participles *injured* and *afflicted* are both predicate adjectives marked in decorating with the wavy line below the word indicating a complement. They are verbals because their sources are the verb stems *to injure* and *to afflict*; they are participles because they are modifying adjectives. Note that these are participles, not participial phrases as we had in verse four. These adjectives could have been written in front of the nouns they modify, but the poet preferred to place them later in the clause as predicate adjectives. Predicate adjectives describe the subject of the verb while predicate nouns rename the subject of the verb.

In Isaiah 1:6b the poet uses three participles to create three haunting images. Verse six in its entirety becomes chilling:

> From the sole of your foot to the top of your head there is no soundness—only wounds and welts and open sores, not cleansed or bandaged or soothed with oil.

The words *wounds* and *welts* and *sores* go along with there being *no soundness*. To add insult to this injury, the cleansing and bandaging and soothing necessary for healing are painfully absent. *Not cleansed, bandaged or soothed* modifies the three nouns: *wounds*, *welts* and *sores*. The writer uses the extended metaphor to show the need for and the absence of care. The participles (*not*) *cleansed, bandaged* and *soothed* seal the fate of the sick body. Please note that the writers of scripture use the tools of grammar, such as participles, to convey that actions have been taken and healing has begun. You and I are not writers of scripture, but we have been called to write correctly and powerfully as servants of our brothers and sisters.

We have looked briefly at gerunds; we have noted a few participles. You may never have seen a gerund or a participle in the Bible before. That's fine. Anita Beaty, on one calm evening, told the Old Testament scholar Walter Brueggemann that Jim Beaty was writing a grammar text and searching for verbals in the Hebrew Bible. My friend, the venerable Brueggeman, laughed heartily and said, "Who but Jim Beaty would be home on a Friday night searching for gerunds?" I said earlier that I do not want the study of grammar to thwart Bible study; however, knowing grammar will make us all better hermeneutists. That said, let us move to the third of the verbals, infinitives.

Infinitives

The third kind of verbal, the infinitive, is identified with the word *to*—the sign of the verb stem. The word *to* plus the stem of the verb form creates the infinitive. Therefore, the infinitive and the verb stem are one and the same, forming the first principal part of every verb.

So the infinitive, like the gerund, is easily recognized. As we now know, the *ing* ending of every gerund makes it easily recognized. And if it is used as a noun, we know it has to be a gerund. Participles can also end with *ing* but may take other forms as well, and they function in sentences either as adjectives or adverbs. Television and radio folks seek our attention with what they term *breaking news*. And poets reach out to us describing the *broken heart*. Both *breaking* and *broken* are participles coming out of verb stems and forming adjectives. Here these participles modify the nouns *news* and *heart*.

The infinitive may function as a noun, an adjective or an adverb. The seventh chapter of Jeremiah, known to many as the Temple Sermon, contains five infinitives in the five following verses: Jeremiah 7:2; 7:10; 7:18; 7:31 and 7:33. In order, the five infinitives are *to worship*, *to do*, *to provide*, *to burn* and *to frighten*.

This treasure of infinitives from Jeremiah's Temple Sermon is found in the following five verses:

> Stand at the gate of the Lord's house and there proclaim this message: Hear the word of the Lord, all you people of Judah who come through these gates **to worship** the Lord. (Jer. 7:2)

In verse two, the infinitive *to worship* introduces the infinitive phrase *to worship the Lord*. This phrase modifies the verb *come*. By now in our study we want to be sure that we break down every phrase within the sentences we read or write.

Jeremiah 7:2b reads,

> Hear the word of the Lord, all you people of Judah who come through the gates **to worship the Lord**.

An independent clause opens the sentence, and a dependent clause closes it. The infinitive phrase *to worship the Lord* ends the sentence and modifies the verb *come* because the phrase tells why the people *come through the gates*. Detailed scrutiny like this is necessary for all editing.

> And then come and stand before me in this house, which bears my Name, and say, "We are safe"—safe **to do** all these detestable things? (Jer. 7:10)

Jeremiah 7:10b, however, contains an infinitive that functions altogether differently from the infinitive in verse two. Its independent clause asks, "'We are safe'—safe to do all these detestable things?" This damning question is addressing an incident when the Lord is quoting what the people have said earlier. Note the neat construction of the infinitive *to do*. It introduces the four words that follow it, making the six-word phrase an infinitive phrase. Thus, words following an infinitive may form an infinitive phrase. We noted in earlier chapters that a phrase is a group of related words that does not contain a subject and a verb. The prepositional phrase is the most frequently used of all phrases, but all three verbals that have accompanying words form phrases. These are called gerund, participial and infinitive phrases

> The children gather wood, the fathers light the fire, and the women knead the dough and make cakes of bread for the Queen of Heaven. They pour out drink offerings to other gods **to provoke** me to anger. (Jer. 7:18)

> They pour out drink offerings to other gods to provoke me to anger. (Jer. 7:18b)

The infinitive phrase *to provoke me to anger* functions as an adverb modifying the verb *pour*.

The infinitives *to burn* (Jer. 7:31a) and *to frighten* (Jer. 7:33b) modify their verbs *have built* and *will be* respectively. These five infinitive phrases function as adverbs, modifying the verbs preceding them.

> They have built the high places of Topheth in the valley of Ben Hinnom, **to burn** their sons and daughters in the fire—something I did not command, nor did it enter my mind.(Jer. 7:31)

> Then the carcasses of this people will become food for the birds of the air and the beasts of the earth, and there will be no one **to frighten** them away. (Jer. 7:33)

Some of the most powerful infinitives in the entire Hebrew Bible and New Testament are found in the classic and beautiful Micah 6:8. That familiar passage reads,

> He has showed you, O man, what is good. And what does the Lord require of you?

This mandate from God to man drives its message home with three infinitive phrases within one long phrase: *to act* justly and *to love* mercy and *to walk* humbly with your God. The poet here writes infinitives to convey clearly a spiritual message to all people. Infinitives work here and infinitives will work in our writing. The three verbals, gerunds, participles and infinitives, increase vocabulary and will add flavor to our writing.

Study Questions for Chapter Nine: A Moment with Verbals

1. How are the Constitution of the United States and the acquaintance with English grammar related?
2. How do some computers respond to the word *verbals*?
3. According to Patricia O'Conner, verbs do what for nouns?
4. Name the three kinds of verbals.
5. Verbals get their life from what?
6. Name the three principal parts of a verb.
7. A gerund always ends with what three letters?
8. A gerund functions as what part of speech?
9. A noun or pronoun that directly precedes a gerund must be written in which one of the three cases?
10. Give an example from scripture when a gerund is a noun, direct object of a verb.
11. What is the difference in the direct object of a verb and a predicate noun?
12. Name the three principal parts of the verb stem *to groan*.
13. Is *to groan* a regular or an irregular verb?
14. In a sentence a participle can be one of two parts of speech. Name them.
15. Why is the word *deadly* in Deuteronomy 32:24 an adjective?
16. Why is the word *deadly* in Deuteronomy 32:24 not a participle?
17. We speak of creating verbals. Explain how this happens.
18. What determines the part of speech of a word in a sentence?
19. Phrases like individual words have parts of speech. A phrase that modifies a noun or a pronoun is what part of speech?
20. A phrase that modifies a verb, adverb or adjective is what part of speech?
21. Isaiah 1:5b contains two participles. Name the two words and tell why they are participles.
22. Isaiah 1:6b contains the words *cleansed, bandaged* and *soothed*. Are these words verbals? What is their part of speech?
23. What little word indicates or announces an infinitive?

24. An infinitive forms which of the three principal parts of a verb?
25. An infinitive can function as any one of the three parts of speech. Name them.
26. Verbals in good writing increase what and add what?

TEN

The Comma

The comma gives everybody fits, and it's no wonder. All punctuation can be troublesome, but I believe the comma causes the most headaches. For years, however, I have watched students move from confusion to confidence in using the comma. I simplify punctuation by introducing four comma rules. Four rules cover all the times we would ever need to write a comma. All uses fit into one of the four following categories. Rule four is a catchall that includes all other comma uses not covered in the first three rules. The first three rules come easy.

Comma Rule Number 1: Place a Comma before a Coordinate Conjunction When That Conjunction Joins Two Independent Clauses

I call this rule the "before" rule: "Place a comma before a coordinate conjunction when that conjunction joins two independent clauses." *Sacred Grammar* has referred often to the seven coordinate conjunctions. The student of this text remembers the acronym FANBOYS: F = for, A = and, N = nor, B = but, O = or, Y = yet and S = so.

Failure to place a comma before or in front of a coordinate conjunction when it joins two independent clauses is not an earth-shattering error. Some good writers ignore this rule; some publishers do not require that this rule be obeyed. But when my students comply with this rule, they indicate that they understand the structure of the sentence. However, the comma (,) written alone between two independent clauses is a serious error, always to be avoided. The comma standing naked between two independent clauses is called the comma splice. It's a thunder clap. It's a dreaded thing. The greatest moment of excitement in the lives of some wrinkled English teachers comes upon uncovering a comma splice. Even the most lenient editor does not permit comma splices. Most English translations of the Bible follow this comma rule in order to avoid comma splices. Another way to avoid the comma splice is to use a semicolon (;) between two independent clauses without a conjunction.

Reading prose passages almost anywhere in the Hebrew Bible or in the New Testament rewards the search for independent clauses separated by the comma in front of a coordinate conjunction (, and). Note that the comma before a coordinate conjunction is written in the space immediately following the last letter of the last word in the previous clause, touching that letter. Daniel 4:12b contains a compound sentence made up of three independent clauses. The first two independent clauses are separated with (, and).

> Under it (the tree in Daniel's dream) the beasts of the field found shelter, and the birds of the air lived in its branches; from it every creature was fed. (Dan. 4:12b)

This verse uses two different marks of punctuation, both correct, between the independent clauses. The first two clauses employ this rule: "Place a comma before a coordinate conjunction when that conjunction joins two independent clauses." The two independent clauses that close this verse have the semicolon as the separator. I cite these three clauses separated by two different marks of punctuation: the comma before the coordinate conjunction in the first instance (*shelter, and*) and the semicolon (*branches; from*) in the second.

Another example of this first comma rule occurs in Acts 1:5.

> For John baptized with water, but in a few days you will be baptized with the Holy Spirit.

Reading only five verses into the book of Acts, the reader finds an example of this same "before" rule where the comma is placed in front of the coordinate conjunction *but*. Again, good writers like the apostle Luke and many others occasionally begin sentences with coordinate conjunctions.

You and I have permission to emulate these good writers. Luke begins the fifth verse of the first chapter of his book with the coordinate conjunction *for*. Make the acronym, FANBOYS, your friend and use it.

State this rule again: "Place a comma before a coordinate conjunction when that conjunction joins two independent clauses." I repeat this rule because I want you to say it again and again. Learn it. Ponder it. Put it under your pillow. Acts 2:32 employs this before rule once again.

> God has raised this Jesus to life, and we are all witnesses of the fact.

This crisp, clear compound sentence uses the first comma rule. We will show a few more verses that employ this rule.

Look at this famous, often quoted verse in Acts 4:12.

> Salvation is found in no one else, for there is no other name under heaven given to men by which we must be saved.

The (*else, for*) construction correctly separates the two independent clauses in this compound-complex sentence. By the way, the group of related words *which we must be saved* is also a clause, as we have learned in earlier chapters. Which of the two kinds of clauses is it? Which word subordinates this clause? And that subordinator is what part of speech? Be sure that you understand how this clause makes the sentence complex in the broader compound-complex sentence definition. Two independent clauses build a compound sentence. Add one or more dependent clauses, and the sentence becomes compound-complex. The last clause is made dependent by the relative pronoun *which*. Note that the word written immediately in front of *which* is the preposition *by*. This entire dependent clause is the object of the preposition *by*. A preposition is one of the eight parts of speech, and it joins its object (a noun or a pronoun) to the rest of the sentence. Not often do we see a prepositional phrase whose object is a clause. This dependent clause acts as the noun object in the prepositional phrase *by which we must be saved*.

Acts 2:32 quoted earlier reads,

> God has raised this Jesus to life, and we are all witnesses to the fact.

With perfect clarity and easy balance, these two independent clauses are joined by the (*life, and*) connection. In the same chapter, Acts 2:43 reads,

> Everyone was filled with awe, and many wonders and miraculous signs were done by the apostles.

The two sentences in Acts 2:32 and Acts 2:43 have the exact pattern. Note in these sentences the clear balance. These verses exemplify the use of comma rule number 1. I remember this rule by referring to it as the "before" rule: "Place a comma before a coordinate conjunction when that conjunction joins two independent clauses." Note well the voice of the verb in the second clause of the sentence quoted above from Acts 2:43. The verb *were done* is passive voice because the subject is *signs*. What was done (*miraculous signs*) is more central to the message of the sentence than the doers of the miracle, thus the passive voice.

Comma Rule Number 2: Place a Comma After a Long Introductory Clause or Phrase.

I refer to comma rule number 2 as the "after" rule. Look carefully at the word *introductory*. Its use here means two things. First, *introductory clause* means that the clause appears at the beginning of the sentence. Second, *introductory clause* also means that the clause at the beginning of the sentence is dependent. Therefore, an introductory clause is a dependent clause that appears at the beginning of the sentence. It depends on another clause to give it life. Without an independent clause following, the dependent clause written in hopes of being a sentence becomes a fragment, which is incorrect. The Acts of the Apostles, like all other good writing, uses this second comma rule. However, before looking at another example, we need to note the word *long* in comma rule number 2. In this rule *long* means six or more words. Marks of punctuation are used for the convenience of the reader. Clear punctuation ensures good manners. The pause after six or more words permits the reader to catch her breath. Therefore, this "after" rule comes into play following long introductory clauses and phrases. Remember that a phrase containing six or more words at the beginning of a sentence also requires a comma following it.

Let's look at this verse from Acts. Please note the reason for the placement of the comma.

> When the day of Pentecost came, they were all together in one place. (Acts 2:1)

Imagine being called on to decorate the first clause in the following sentence:

> While the beggar held on to Peter and John, all the people were astonished and came running to them in the place called Solomon's Colonnade. (Acts 3:11)

Remember that the first task in decorating a sentence is to locate and underline every verb using two straight lines. Always begin with the verb. In this instance the verb is the word *came*. The first two steps of the "clause test" require finding the verb and then finding its subject. This subject-verb cluster forms the clause. In step three we determine the kind of clause, independent or dependent. If a subordinator (a subordinate conjunction or a relative pronoun) appears immediately in front of the subject-verb cluster, the clause is dependent. If no subordinator appears, the clause is independent.

Look again at Acts 2:1, "When the day of Pentecost came, they were all together in one place." The first six words of Acts 2:1 form a clause. That clause is *introductory* because the word *when* appears in front of the subject-verb cluster (*day/came*). The New International Version (NIV) places a comma after the sixth word *came*. Marks of punctuation exist as an effort to aid the reader. Correct punctuation helps to build clear, crisp sentences. The second clause in Acts 2:1, "they were all together in one place," completes the complex sentence as it is an independent clause, having no subordinator in front of the subject-verb cluster. An independent clause and a dependent clause make a complex sentence.

Look again at Acts 3:11.

> While the beggar held on to Peter and John, all the people were astonished and came running to them in the place called Solomon's Colonnade.

Using sentences from the Bible to teach grammar is an honor. As I cite the various verses, I often opt, for the sake of time and space, not to comment on the context of the verse or its passage. However, here, I am compelled to note the context of Acts 3:11. In this verse the beggar holds on to Peter and John. A beggar mind you. Peter has healed this man who has spent a lifetime begging at a gate called Beautiful. The beggar has already leaped for joy because suddenly he can walk. The context describing this event teaches apposite rules for living. Early in this passage the people go up into the temple to pray at three o'clock in the afternoon. The beggar, crippled from birth, is taken every day to the gate, Beautiful. Every day, good people carry him there. Evidently, he has lived for years on what temple dwellers have seen fit to give him. As Peter and John are about to enter the temple, this beggar asks them for money.

Was Begging Permitted In Jerusalem?

Apparently, the City of Jerusalem permits begging. The exchange between these three people involves their eyes. Both Peter and John look straight at the beggar. Some years ago when Atlanta, "the city too busy to hate," began its purging of homeless people, a spokesperson representing the city's position on "the quality of life" ordinances spoke to a group of women in a prominent corporate office. The speaker's first word of advice to the women if they encountered homeless people was, "Don't look them in the eye." The speaker went on to explain that the ambassadors, a corps of civilian monitors, were on call to summon police if arrests for begging were necessary.

Neither Peter nor John called either the ambassadors or the police. These two preachers made eye contact with the unwashed beggar. Peter not only "looked straight at him" (Acts 3:4), but also told the beggar, cripple from birth, to "look at us." Wanting money, the beggar gave his full attention. Imagine, two preachers on the streets of Jerusalem, or on any other street, having no money. But Peter has no money. He follows with perhaps the most powerful statement in the passage. "But what I have I give you." Unfortunately, the strength that comes to the beggar's ankles gets all the press. We attend to the dramatic and to the startling. His hooting and hollering and jumping and praising make for good television, even for good worship in some circles. But the power that Peter and John bring goes beyond the spectacular. The power lies in the fact that these preachers gave what they had—themselves. Most of us will not cause the lame to walk nor the blind to see. But each of us has the opportunity, the high privilege, to give ourselves to individuals in need and to each other. That is the greater miracle in this powerful passage. The faith of the beggar initiates the process whose miraculous conclusion is *complete healing* (Acts 3:16). His faith, his initiative, his energy, his determination, his confidence all roll into one force that results in wonder. What a life lesson for each of us.

> By faith in the name of Jesus, this man whom you see and know was made strong. (Acts 3:16a)

Again, the comma rule that we are discussing states, "Place a comma after a long introductory clause or phrase." Be clear that the comma after *Jesus* (,) is placed there adhering to this rule.

Of course, this rule applies to both dependent clauses that contain six or more words and to phrases that contain six or more words. Observing these two comma rules requires the knowledge of sentence structure. Structure implies building. And sentences are built with clauses. The first rule, the before rule, addresses the punctuation between independent clauses. The second rule, the after rule, addresses the punctuation that follows long introductory (dependent) clauses and phrases. The next two rules are more stylistic than the *before* and *after* rules.

Before discussing the final two comma rules, I want to share one writer's happy view of the importance of the placing of commas and periods. Lynne Truss in her book, *Eats, Shoots & Leaves*, says, "It's tough being a stickler for punctuation these days" (2). A few pages later she compares two different sentences showing the results of what she calls "mispunctuation" or "re-punctuation" (9). The sentences are the following:

> A woman, without her man, is nothing.
> A woman: without her, man is nothing.

As we can see punctuation can drastically alter the meaning of a series of words, even to the point of creating two sentences with completely opposite meanings.

Look at the two versions of the "Dear Jack" letter quoted from pages nine and ten.

Dear Jack,

I want a man who knows what love is all about. You are generous, kind, thoughtful. People who are not like you admit to being useless and inferior. You have ruined me for other men. I yearn for you. I have no feelings whatsoever when we're apart. I can be forever happy—will you let me be yours?

Jill

The second "Dear Jack" letter with the same words but different punctuation is another read. Note the huge contrast.

Dear Jack:

I want a man who knows what love is. All about you are generous, kind, thoughtful people, who are not like you. Admit to being useless and inferior. You have ruined me. For other men I yearn. For you I have no feelings whatsoever. When we're apart I can be forever happy. Will you let me be?

Yours,

Jill

The second letter expresses animosity and resentment. The first conveys love and affection. The word order of the two letters is identical; only the punctuation is different. The examples cited here are extreme, even absurd. However, these examples drive home the point that punctuation changes meaning.

Comma Rule Number 3: Words or Groups of Words in a Series

The third occasion that calls for using a comma is easily understood: "Place a comma after words or groups of words in a series." For example,

On that very day Noah and his sons, Shem, Ham and Japheth, together with his wife and the wives of his three sons, entered into the ark. (Gen. 7:13)

You were in Eden, the garden of God; every precious stone adorned you: ruby, topaz and emerald, chrysolite, onyx and jasper, sapphire, turquoise and beryl. (Ezek. 28:13)

I use the following phrases to teach the use of the comma to separate groups of phrases in a sentence: in the cloud, over the cloud, under the cloud, beside the cloud, with the cloud, through the cloud and around the cloud.

These three-word phrases are all prepositional phrases where the preposition joins its object to the rest of the sentence. The first five groups of words form a series and, according to our rule, need to have commas following them. But no comma appears between the last two, "through the cloud and around the cloud."

Comma Rule Number 4: Nonrestrictive Elements, Parenthetical Expressions, Interrupters, Appositives, Etc.

Before approaching the terms listed above, let's review briefly the three comma rules. Comma rule number 1, the *before* rule, states, "Place a comma before (in front of) a coordinate conjunction when that conjunction joins two independent clauses." Remember that a comma written between two independent clauses, without a coordinating conjunction preceding it, creates a comma splice. A comma splice is always a serious punctuation error and must be avoided.

Comma rule number 2, the *after* rule, states, "Place a comma after a long introductory clause or phrase." In this rule the words *long* and *introductory* sometimes confuse unless we know that *long* means six or more words (6+); *introductory* refers to a dependent clause that comes at the beginning of the sentence.

Comma rule number 3, discussed recently, states, "Place a comma after words or groups of words in a series." These three uses or rules for writing commas are cut and dried.

The fourth comma rule, as we cite it in this text, covers all other instances of comma usage. Working from only four comma rules makes for convenience. However, rule four is a catchall because it covers so many different uses of the comma. My students like to say that this fourth rule covers "a multitude of sins."

Recently, I received a complimentary copy of a text entitled *The Thompson Handbook*, edited by David Blakesley and Jeffrey L. Hoogeveen, soon to be published by Thomson Wadsworth of Boston. The book contains 1045 pages not counting its glossary, an index and two inside-the-back-cover pages. A volume like this one is a resource that every person should consult. However, the beginner who does not know that a comma splice is an error feels overwhelmed trying to sort out all the different comma rules cited in this text. This is my reason for following the lead of other grammar instructors who teach only four comma rules. By combining the majority of comma usages under this fourth rule, we have, I pray, made the road a bit smoother. Let us revisit the heading of this section in order to discuss comma rule number 4:

"Nonrestrictive Elements, Parenthetical Expressions, Interrupters, Appositives, Etc."

We come now to the writing of commas where the placing is not as cut and dried as in the first three rules. But after we have looked at examples, these commas under rule four will be as clear as their cousins in the first three rules. Remember we call those the *before*, *after* and *series* comma rules. This fourth rule addresses all other instances where commas are used.

Nonrestrictive Elements

A *nonrestrictive element* is a word, phrase or dependent clause that gives information not essential to understanding the basic message of the element it modifies and, therefore, is set off with commas. But it makes sense, before exploring nonrestrictive elements, to take a brief look at the restrictive element.

Restrictive Elements

A word, phrase or dependent clause that contains information essential to understanding the message of the sentence is a *restrictive element*. I want to use a sentence that contains a restrictive element that my students grasp readily: Anyone *who walks a mile every day* will live to be eighty-years-old.

The restrictive element in this complex sentence is the dependent clause *who walks a mile every day*. Note that no commas surround this clause because it is necessary to the meaning of the sentence. This dependent clause is a relative clause that is subordinated by the relative pronoun *who*, which also serves as the subject of the clause. No commas set off restrictive or necessary elements. The clause *who walks a mile every day* carries the meaning of the sentence. The restrictive element contains essential information that carries the message of the sentence.

1 Corinthians 2:9b contains one restrictive clause as Paul alludes to Isaiah 64:4:

> No mind has conceived what **God has prepared** for those who love him. (1 Cor. 2:9b)

The clause in **bold** carries the message of the verse; it is restrictive/necessary and has no commas surrounding it.

> Anyone **who** claims **to be a king** opposes Caesar. (John 19:12)

Claiming to be a king labels *anyone* as an opponent to Caesar. The clause is restrictive/necessary and needs no commas. Exodus 21:12 contains one restrictive clause, written in **bold** letters:

> Anyone **who strikes a man and kills him** shall surely be put to death.

Examples of Nonrestrictive Elements

Look at the nonrestrictive clause in 2 Corinthians 11:31:

> The God and Father of the Lord Jesus, **who is to be praised forever,** knows that I am not lying.

The dependent relative clause, however important, does not carry the thrust of the sentence; it is unessential information modifying *God* and is surrounded with commas. Jeremiah 44:24 contains a nonrestrictive phrase that is set off with commas.

> Then Jeremiah said to all the people, **including the women,** "Hear the word of the Lord, all you people of Judah in Egypt."

The phrase in **bold** type is important, but again, it gives information not essential to the message of the sentence.

> Noah was a righteous man, **blameless among the people of his time,** and he walked with God. (Gen. 6:9b)

The nonrestrictive element in this sentence is "blameless among the people of his time," and it is set off with or surrounded by commas. Again, the message of the sentence tells that Noah is a righteous man who walked with God. Being "blameless among the people of his time" is both important and noteworthy; however, it is added information. Therefore, it is set off with or surrounded by commas because it is nonrestrictive.

Another example of a nonrestrictive dependent clause is Genesis 11:10b:

> Two years after the flood, **when Shem was one hundred years old,** he became the father of Arphaxad.

This portion of the verse states that a man named Shem fathered a son named Arphaxad two years after the flood. The nonrestrictive element in this sentence adds the information that "when he was one hundred years old" Arphaxad became a father. The dependent clause is set off or surrounded with commas; it is not the essential message of the sentence. Mature gentlemen might marvel at the contents of this nonrestrictive clause; nevertheless, the core message of the sentence reports Shem's becoming a father after the flood.

> So he built an altar there to the Lord, **who had appeared to him.** (Gen. 12:7b)

The dependent clause at the end of this sentence is a relative clause used as an adjective that modifies the noun *Lord*. The clause at the end of the sentence is nonrestrictive because it adds extra information. The text correctly sets off this nonrestrictive element with the comma.

> The whole land of Canaan, **where you are now an alien,** I will give as an everlasting possession to you and your descendants after you; and I will be their God. (Gen. 17:8)

The nonrestrictive dependent clause is set off with commas. It modifies the proper noun *Canaan*; it provides additional information. The powerful message says that the whole of Canaan will be given as an everlasting possession to the children of Israel and to their descendants. How preposterous! And the Lord promises to be their God. The nonrestrictive element gives the extra information about their present state. Please note the commas before and after the clause. Imagine a voiceless, oppressed, maligned group of homeless men, women and children in a downtown shelter being told by God that they would one day own Atlanta's City Hall. And a bonus is added, "and I will be their God." We can learn how truth speaks to power from the writings of scripture.

Example of a nonrestrictive participial phrase:

> He prepared a meal for them, **baking bread without yeast**, and they ate. (Gen. 19:3b)

The message of this crisp sentence is twofold: Lot prepared a meal, and two angels ate it. The information that the bread was baked without yeast carries significance and vital symbolism. But the preparing and eating the meal is the message. The extra information telling how the bread was baked is set off or surrounded by commas because it is not essential to the message of the sentence. The phrase is a participial phrase used as an adverb modifying the verb *prepared*. Participles are usually adjectives, but here the participial phrase functions as an adverb.

Example of a nonrestrictive dependent clause:

> Then the angel of God, **who had been traveling in front of Israel's army,** withdrew and went behind them. (Exod. 14:19)

That the angel of God withdrew and followed behind them is the message of the sentence. The relative clause *who had been traveling in front of Israel's army* modifies the noun *angel*. Adjectives modify nouns; therefore, this dependent clause functions as an adjective modifying the noun *angel*. Whether the angel of the Lord leads or follows, protection is the message. The position of the angel ahead or behind symbolizes surrounding support.

Example of a nonrestrictive dependent clause:

> Do not worship any other God, for the Lord, **whose name is Jealous,** is a jealous God. (Exod. 34:14)

We need to call up our decorating skills in order to investigate the clauses in this sentence. Were we decorating this verse we would underline twice the complete verb in the first clause, *do . . . worship*. No subject of that verb is present; its subject is the understood, *you*. There is no subordinator; therefore, the clause is independent. The comma and then the coordinating conjunction *for* indicate that an independent clause follows. Remember the comma rule that states, "Place a comma before [in front of] a coordinate conjunction when the conjunction joins two independent clauses." Two independent clauses are joined here by the coordinate conjunction *for*.

The second independent clause following the coordinate conjunction reads, "The Lord . . . is a jealous God." So far, these two independent clauses would make the sentence compound. But note the ellipsis above. The words *whose name is Jealous* are set off or surrounded by commas because this four-word dependent clause forms a nonrestrictive element. This dependent clause makes the sentence compound-complex, having two independent clauses and one dependent clause. Be sure that you understand the commas in each of the previously quoted verses: Genesis 6:9b, Genesis 11:10b, Genesis 12:7b, Genesis 17:8, Genesis 19:3b, Genesis 14:19 and Exodus 34:14. Each of these seven verses contains a nonrestrictive element. A nonrestrictive element is a word or group of words that is not needed to convey the meaning of the sentence; therefore, it is set off or surrounded by commas.

The Thomson Handbook explains the nonrestrictive element as "a word group that is not essential to the core meaning of the sentence . . . . You can omit a nonrestrictive element from a sentence without changing its main idea. Nonrestrictive elements are often (but not always) signaled by the words *which* and *who*" (929).

A parenthetical expression is typically a word or phrase, not a clause or an appositive. Parenthetical expressions are set off with commas because they are not needed to convey the meaning of the sentence. Exodus 16:27 gives an example of a parenthetical expression,

> Nevertheless, some of the people went out on the seventh day to gather it, but they found none.

More of the same follows in Jeremiah 33:6.

> Nevertheless, I will bring health and healing to it; I will heal my people and let them enjoy abundant peace and security.

Paul uses a parenthetical expression in the middle of 2 Corinthians 13:5b:

> Do you not realize that Christ Jesus is in you—unless, **of course**, you fail the test?

And note the similar punctuation in these two verses:

> **In that day,** a man will keep alive a young cow and two goats. (Isa. 7:21)

> **In that day,** in every place where there were a thousand vines worth a thousand silver shekels, there will be only briars and thorns. (Isa. 7:23)

The prepositional phrase *in that day* in each of these verses in the NIV translation is considered to be a parenthetical expression set off with commas. It is a parenthetical expression in both verses because without it the messages contained in the two verses remain the same. Some translations, such as the New Revised Standard Version (NRSV), place no commas, considering the phrase to be essential to carry the meaning of the sentence. As in a few other instances whenever considering the placement of commas, the writer has a choice.

Appositives

An appositive is a noun, a noun phrase or a noun clause that renames a noun or a pronoun next to it. The decision to place commas around appositives or appositive phrases is determined usually by whether the *appositive* or *appositive phrase* is restrictive or nonrestrictive.

Nonrestrictive Appositives

Example: George W. Bush, *our forty-third president*, holds degrees from Yale and Harvard.

The appositive phrase *our forty-third president* is nonrestrictive as it is not essential to carry the core message of the sentence. That Mr. Bush is the forty-third president is information worth noting, but the message of the sentence focuses on his degrees and the universities where he earned them. The commas set off the nonrestrictive phrase, *our forty-third president.*

Example: This is Jesus, **the King of the Jews.** (Matt. 27:37)
Example: And Stephen, **full of grace and power,** was performing great wonders and signs among the people. (Acts 6:8)
Example: Cyprus, the **leader of the synagogue,** and all his household believed in the Lord. (Acts 18:8a)
Example: The word of the Lord is against you, **O Canaan,** land of the Philistines. (Zeph. 2:5)

In the three previous examples, *our forty-third president, the King of the Jews, full of grace and power, the leader of the synagogue* and *O Canaan* are nonrestrictive elements that need to be set off with commas.

Restrictive Appositives

No commas adorn restrictive elements. The following example comes from Genesis 27:20b:

The Lord **your God** gave me success, he replied.

This seven word quote comes from the mouth of Jacob as he pretends to be his older brother, Esau. The words *your God* are restrictive as they identify the particular God who is the Lord of old Isaac.

> When the disciples **James and John** saw this, they asked, "Lord, do you want us to call fire down from heaven and destroy them? (Luke 9:54)

The names of *James and John* distinguish the two particular disciples that asked the question. These names are restrictive and need to be present in the sentence; without them, all the disciples would be asking the question.

The following sentence is another example of a restrictive appositive: Jonathan Weiner's book *The Beak of the Finch* won a Pulitzer Prize. *The Beak of the Finch* has no commas around it. As the title of the prize-winning novel, it is restrictive and setting it off with commas would be incorrect. Restrictive elements are not surrounded by commas. If I placed commas around *The Beak of the Finch,* I would be saying that the title could be left out of the sentence without changing the meaning. Not so. Leave off the commas. Appositives surrounded by commas are nonrestrictive and come under the category that we have labeled comma rule four. This fourth rule is misnamed. This fourth category is not a rule at all; it is rather a catchall. Comma usage not covered in the first three comma rules falls into rule four, the catchall category.

Commas with Introductory Elements

Examples:

Introductory words, like *however* that serve as interrupters, are often set off by commas.

> **However,** God has not allowed him to harm me. (Gen. 31:7b)

Note: If the interjection is emphatic it can be set off with an exclamation point instead of a comma. The choice belongs to the writer.

> Woe to you, O land whose king was a servant and whose princes feast in the morning. (Eccles. 10:15)

> And again they shouted: **Hallelujah!** the smoke from her goes up forever and ever. (Rev. 19:3)

Commas before a Nonrestrictive Relative Clause

> From the basket of bread made without yeast, **which is before the Lord**, take a loaf, and a cake made with oil, and a wafer. (Exod. 29:23)

The relative pronoun *which* builds the dependent clause. It must be set off with the comma because it is nonrestrictive. So often a *which* clause that follows an independent clause needs the comma right in front of it.

> I will wipe mankind, whom I have created, from the face of the earth. (Gen. 6:7)

Commas with Transitional Expressions

> If, **in fact,** Abraham was justified by works, he had something to boast about—but not before God. (Rom. 4:2)

Commas with Quotations

> They stayed at a distance and said to Moses, "Speak to us yourself and we will listen. But do not have God speak to us or we will die." (Exod. 20:18b)

> "There, in the tent**,**" he said. (Gen. 18:6b)

> He said, "Cursed be Canaan!" (Gen. 9:25)

Note that the explanation point and the comma are inside the quotation marks.

Commas in Addresses

When the street, city and state are run together in a line; commas are needed in the address. However, do not set off the zip code.

Example:

> 1024 Washington Street, Columbia, SC 29205

Example:

> 477 Peachtree Street, Atlanta, GA 30308

Commas in Place Names

Example:

> My friends from Kenya attend Beulah Heights University, Atlanta, Georgia.

Example:

> The state capitol is located in Raleigh, North Carolina.

Commas in Months and Days in the Year

Example:

> William Shakespeare died on April 23, 1616.

Example:

> The English beheaded Charles I on January 30, 1649.

Example:

> The English beheaded Charles I on 30 January 1649.

Note: If the day precedes the month, no comma is necessary.

Commas in Long Numbers

Example: 18,325
485,667
92,000,000

Commas set off long numbers in groups of three beginning from the right. In four-digit numbers the comma is optional.

Example:
6,491 or 6491

As long as people create sentences, placing commas will present challenges. Placing commas everywhere signifies a disease that I have lovingly named "commaitis." The Latin *itis* means *inflammation*. Avoid commaitis by learning when *not* to use commas. I ask my students to help me avoid inflammation. On the other hand, the failure to punctuate with commas when needed can be just as costly. Both extremes, too many or too few, must be avoided in good writing.

Following the steps set out in this chapter will help you avoid many comma errors.

Self-Quiz for Chapter Ten: The Comma

1. Which punctuation mark gives most trouble?
2. What very well may be the most frequently committed punctuation error?
3. Which comma rule is the most frequently used?
4. What is the *after* comma rule?
5. Explain a comma splice; what is it?
6. When following the *before* comma rule, where precisely is the comma written or typed?
7. State the *before* comma rule.
8. Write the seven coordinate conjunctions we learn from FANBOYS.

9. Define a preposition.
10. Why is the *after* comma rule called the *after* rule? What is after what?
11. Define an introductory clause.
12. What mark of punctuation can replace the comma and coordinate conjunction that separates two independent clauses?
13. The comma rule that states, "*long introductory clauses*" refers to the number of words in a dependent clause. What number is long?
14. Define a complex sentence.
15. Did Jerusalem allow begging on its streets?
16. Does Atlanta allow begging on its streets?
17. Define a compound sentence.
18. What do the two "Dear Jack" letters show us?
19. Define a compound-complex sentence.
20. Why is comma rule four a "ringer"?
21. Define a *nonrestrictive* element.
22. Are *nonrestrictive* words, phrases or dependent clauses set off with commas?
23. Define a *restrictive* element.
24. Are *restrictive* words, phrases or dependent clauses set off with commas?
25. Why is *who walks every day* in the example given in this chapter restrictive?
26. Exodus 34:14 gives God a rather unusual name. What is it?
27. Nonrestrictive elements are often (but not always) signaled by what two pronouns?
28. What kind of pronouns are those mentioned in number 27?
29. Define parenthetical expressions.
30. How do *Sacred Grammar* and *The Thomson Handbook* disagree on the *series* comma rule?
31. How does *Hodges' Harbrace Handbook* define appositive?
32. How does *The Thomson Handbook* define appositive?
33. Is a zip code that follows the name of the state in an address set off with commas?
34. Write a sentence that shows the month, day and year of William Shakespeare's death.
35. The made-up word *commaitis* describes what punctuation error?

ELEVEN

Writing That Paper

Teachers of public speaking know that many people fear talking in front of an audience, large or small. Some speakers experience such fear that they would rather parachute from a plane than deliver a speech. Not far behind that crowd stands another group, people who are frightened at the prospect of writing a paper to be read and graded by a teacher. Usually English classes more than any other scholastic discipline require written papers. But writing papers cannot be avoided.

This *Sacred Grammar* text emphasizes clear writing using the Bible as its example. We have looked at the kinds of sentences according to structure, like the complex sentences in Judges, John and Mark. We have reviewed the eight parts of speech; for example, we looked at verbs in 2 Kings. We have worked with aspects of grammar ranging from the cases of nouns to the principal parts of verbs. We have labored with the nuances of punctuation. We learned rules and their usage in biblical writing to reach this point: learning to write easily and clearly.

Sometimes my students cite the great Samuel Johnson who once said that writing was such drudgery that it should be avoided except to earn money. My students tell me that people make money, get rich, and preach great sermons without having to write papers for English classes. I got so weary of hearing their complaints that I decided to use the Holy Bible to show them that scripture adheres to rules of clarity and consistency. So I return to my soapbox to say that by taking a few deliberate steps, we can together turn the task of writing into a pleasant experience.

Biblical Writers on Writing

Repeatedly, the writers and translators of the Hebrew Bible and the New Testament emphasize the importance of concise, clear, correct expression.

Exodus 17:14a gives a command to write:

> Then the Lord said to Moses, Write this on a scroll as something to be remembered.

This command follows Joshua's defeating the Amalekite army. The victory occurs as Moses holds up both hands. Whenever Moses lowers his hands the Amalekites gain the advantage; whenever he raises his hands the Israelites take the advantage. Aaron and Hur stand beside Moses, until sunset, and hold up his hands for him, assuring victory. In order for this strange incident to be remembered, God commands that it be written for safekeeping on a scroll. In that manner the story is preserved for posterity.

One more time, God says to write it down in order to remember it. This remarkable event is preserved by writing it down.

> The Lord says to Moses, chisel out two stone tablets like the first ones, and I will write on them the words that were on the first tablets, which you broke. (Exod. 34:1)

Moses returned from Mount Sinai only to find his people worshipping the golden calf. Infuriated, Moses broke the tablets to pieces. They were written again by God himself. So as the Bible teaches us, even God writes.

Deuteronomy 6:9 reiterates the importance of recalling the Lord's commandments.

> Write them on the doorframes of your houses and on your gates.

The people are about to cross over into the land of milk and honey, promised to their fathers. Deuteronomy 6:4-9 proclaims the following:

> Hear, O Israel: the Lord our God, the Lord is one. Love the Lord your God with all your heart and with all your

soul and with all your strength. These commandments that I give you today are to be upon your hearts. Impress them on your children. Talk about them when you sit at home and when you walk along the road, when you lie down and when you get up. Tie them as symbols on your hands and bind them on your foreheads. Write them on the doorframes of your houses and on your gates.

God's instructions require both literal and figurative imprinting of words—on hearts and on doorframes. The writing of the words seals the deal. Writing them preserves them. Writing them assures their being remembered. The book of Deuteronomy had to be written, written down, because human beings forget. By writing we remember. I tell my students that the sweetest writing they will ever do will be that writing that is about and for the people they love most. Recalling precious memories is one of life's sweetest treasures. Write down those memories. God knows that God's love is impressed on us with words.

Even the King Must Write a Copy of the Law

The last seven verses of Deuteronomy 17 instruct the king how he is to rule and how he is to behave. According to Deuteronomy 17:18 the king is commanded to write. What a different world we would have if all kings, all heads of state, all leaders of government followed this command:

> When he takes the throne of his kingdom, he is to write for himself on a scroll a copy of this law, taken from that of the priests, who are Levites. (Deut. 17:18)

Note that the king writes for himself a copy of this law. The king who is set over the people must know the law, and he is to be held accountable to it. A step toward his inculcating the law is his act of writing it for himself. Imagine the famine, graft, greed, heartache, hunger, lies, murder, pestilence and sorrow that would disappear from the earth if all presidents, monarchs and all other heads of state would write and obey the law set down on the stones as given in the Hebrew Bible.

Written in Stone

Deuteronomy 27:2-3 directs the leaders to write the laws on stones upon crossing Jordan into the land the Lord is giving to them.

> When you have crossed the Jordan into the land the Lord your God is giving you, set up some large stones and coat them with plaster. Write on them all the words of this law when you have crossed over to enter the land the Lord your God is giving you, a land flowing with milk and honey, just as the Lord, the God of your fathers, promised you.

Similar is the message in Deuteronomy 27:8.

> And you shall write very clearly all the words of this law on these stones you have set up.

God requires that all the words of this law be written on stones. The permanence of the words allows all posterity to obey the command to read them. Deuteronomy 27:8 demands that the words be written "very clearly," free of ambiguity.

Deuteronomy 31:19 commands that the words also be sung.

> Now write down for yourselves this song and teach it to the Israelites and have them sing it, so that it may be a witness for me against them.

This became the famous Song of Moses found in Deuteronomy 32:1-43. Moses spoke all the words of this song in the hearing of the people. But this song was penned before it was spoken. There would have been no singing had the words not been written down.

Descriptive Writing Prior to Entering the Promise Land

The book of Joshua contains dozens of verses that mention writing. I cite only one, Joshua 18:4, because Joshua himself ordered a particular kind of writing for a reason.

> Appoint three men from each tribe. I will send them out to make a survey of the land and to write a description of it, according to the inheritance of each. Then they will return to me.

Those of us who want to write well and who thrill at quality writing enjoy the imperatives of this verse: God through Joshua tells three people from each tribe to survey the newly found territory, to write a description of it and to return with their findings. One of the three chosen from each tribe had to be a writer who could capture the beauty, the opportunities, the wealth, and the dangers of the land in a way that enabled others to "see" what each writer saw. Each committee of three made possible the entering and the possessing of the land by means of its written description.

Writing down the events in the book of Jeremiah moves the plot. Some of the powerful people standing around King Jehoiakim when they hear the reading of the scroll, the written word, fear for the safety of Baruch and Jeremiah. The words, dictated by Jeremiah and written in ink by Baruch (Jeremiah 36), foretell the demise of both Jerusalem and her corrupt king, Jehoiakim. Retaliation always follows when truth speaks to power. This powerful plot-moving retaliation is recorded in Jeremiah 36:22-26.

> It was the ninth month, and the king was sitting in the winter house and there was a fire burning in the brazier before him. As Jehudi read three or four columns (of the scroll), the king would cut them off with a penknife and throw them into the fire in the brazier, until the entire scroll was consumed in the fire that was in the brazier. Yet neither the king, nor any of his servants who heard all these words, were afraid, nor did they rend their garments. Even when Elnathan and Delaiah and Gemariah urged the king not to burn the scroll, he would not listen to them. And the king commanded Jerahmeel the king's son and Seraiah . . .

to seize Baruch the secretary and Jeremiah the prophet, but the Lord hid them. (Revised Standard Version)

But these words, Jeremiah's words, written on the scroll and burned by the king in his fireplace, prompt the punishments that follow Jeremiah for the rest of his life. More words were to come as Jeremiah 36:27-32 reports the following:

Now, after the king had burned the scroll with the words that Baruch wrote at Jeremiah's dictation, the word of the Lord came to Jeremiah: Take another scroll and write on it all the former words that were in the first scroll, which King Jehoiakim of Judah has burned. And concerning King Jehoiakim of Judah you shall say: Thus says the Lord, You have dared to burn this scroll, saying, Why have you written in it that the king of Babylon will certainly come and destroy this land, and will cut off from it human beings and animals? Therefore thus says the Lord concerning King Jehoiakim of Judah: he shall have no one to sit upon the throne of David, and his dead body shall be cast out to the heat by day and the frost by night. And I will punish him and his offspring and his servants for their iniquity; I will bring on them, and on the inhabitants of Jerusalem, and on the people of Judah, all the disasters with which I have threatened them - - but they would not listen.

Then Jeremiah took another scroll and gave it to the secretary Baruch son of Neriah, who wrote on it at Jeremiah's dictation all the words of the scroll that King Jehoikim of Judah had burned in the fire; and many similar words were added to them. (New Revised Standard Version)

Jeremiah wrote again everything that he had written before the brazier burning; Jeremiah 36:32b says, "And many similar words were added to them." Every turn of every page reminds the reader the necessity of clear, correctly written words.

Psalms points to poetry as the writing of the tongue, the spoken work. Psalm 45:1b says, "My tongue is the pen of a skillful writer." The poet is a singer and writes words that will be put to music.

> My heart is stirred by a noble theme as I recite my verses for the king; my tongue is the pen of a skilful writer.

The poet recites his verses for the king and while he speaks them, his heart is stirred by a noble theme. Then follows the unlikely metaphor that says his tongue is the pen of a skillful writer. The product of a skillful writer is quality writing. The pen transfers the noble theme from the heart to the page. And the written word imprints the word on the page or on the stone or on the doorframe onto the heart. It is the splendor of this reciprocity that demonstrates the power of language.

New Testament Writers on Writing

The New Testament writers depend also on the power of the written word. It informs; it reforms; it preserves. In his introduction to the third synoptic Gospel, Luke writes,

> Therefore, since I myself have carefully investigated everything from the beginning, it seemed good also to me to write an orderly account for you, most excellent Theophilus, so that you may know the certainty of the things you have been taught. (Luke 1:3-4)

Obviously, Luke wants to assure Theophilus that the teachings he has received are sound. Luke wants to preserve for posterity the findings of his investigation. Luke wants to pen *an orderly account* confirming that quality writing is his standard (Luke 1:3b). He insists that the order of the events is important to remember, and writing confirms and preserves that order. Writing those things is the confirmation of learning.

Jesus Writes a Few Words

In John 8 when the teachers of the law and the Pharisees bring into the Temple a woman caught in the act of adultery, they confront Jesus by quoting the Law of Moses. They want to stone her. Jesus wants to protect her. They use the law. He uses words, written and spoken. When the lawyers and Pharisees continue to ask him questions, he bends down and writes with his finger on the ground. What did he write? We can only surmise. Some believe he wrote on the ground what he was about to say,

> If any one of you is without sin, let him be the first to throw a stone at her. (John 8:7b)

After these nineteen words fell on the ears of the hearers, he stooped down and wrote on the ground again. Don't miss the power of this masterful man. He sandwiched what he said by writing before he spoke and after he spoke. He stoops and writes; he stands and speaks. He punctuates his spoken words with a second writing. The old fellows present were the first to drop their rocks, their weapons of death. They remembered, and they left. Jesus' writing on the ground levels the field. He reverses our attention from the accused to the accusers. His manipulation focuses on the communal sin rather than the individual's missing of the mark. All have sinned, and all have fallen short of the mark, but the community's scapegoating the accused backfires on them all.

The Written Word Carries Power

The chief priests of the Jews in John 19:21 attempt to edit Pilate's words, "Do not write the King of the Jews, but that this man claimed to be the king of the Jews." These priests know that the written word carries power. They want no possibility of misinterpretation, a failure to discern between an actual king and one who only claims to be a king.

The writer of Hebrews creates a metaphor that shows where the Lord will write his message. In Hebrews 8:10b the Lord declares that he will "put my laws in their minds and write them on their hearts." The metaphor of writing the law on their hearts conveys a sealing of the covenant that has been established between the Lord and his people. Hebrews 10:15-16 expresses the same thought, but in this instance, the Lord speaks of the Holy Spirit and declares,

> The Holy Spirit also testifies to us about this. First he says, This is the covenant I will make with them after that time, says the Lord. I will put my laws in their hearts, and I will write them on their minds.

Note that the surface for the writing is metaphorically *their minds.* God constantly uses the image of writing as both literal and figurative. We see writing on a surface, and we then can imagine the words as imprinted literally on our hearts and minds.

Botching the Biblical Context

The attitude that a writer brings to a topic makes all the difference in the written paper. For topics, I often assign Bible verses, sometimes full passages from the Bible. Recently I asked for an in-class, impromptu writing. My assignment to a class of twenty-five freshmen writers was to write an interpretation of Isaiah 1:18 in its context. Each person had a Bible available. For its literary beauty I directed them to the first eighteen verses of the first chapter of Isaiah.

> The vision concerning Judah and Jerusalem that Isaiah son of Amoz saw during the reigns of Uzziah, Jotham, Ahaz, and Hezekiah, kings of Judah. Hear, O heavens! Listen O earth! For the Lord has spoken: "I reared children and brought them up, but they have rebelled against me. The ox knows his master, the donkey his owner's manger, but Israel does not know, my people do not understand." Ah, sinful nation, a people loaded with guilt, a brood of evildoers, children given to corruption! They have forsaken the Lord; they have spurned the Holy One of Israel and turned their backs on him. Why should you be beaten any more? Why do you persist in rebellion? Your whole head is injured, your whole heart afflicted. From the sole of your foot to the top of your head there is no soundness—only wounds and welts and open sores, not cleansed or bandaged or soothed with oil. Your country is desolate, your cities burned with fire; your fields are being stripped by foreigners right before you, laid waste as when overthrown by strangers. The Daughter of Zion is left like a shelter in a vineyard, like a hut in a field of melons, like a city under siege. Unless the Lord Almighty had left us some survivors, we would have become like Sodom, we would have been like Gomorrah. Hear the word of the Lord, you

rulers of Sodom; listen to the law of our God, you people of Gomorrah! "The multitude of your sacrifices—what are they to me?" says the Lord. "I have more than enough of your burnt offering, of rams and the fat of fattened animals; I have no pleasure in the blood of bulls and lambs and goats. When you come to appear before me, who has asked this of you, this trampling of my courts? Stop bringing meaningless offerings! Your incense is detestable to me. New Moons, Sabbaths and convocations—I cannot bear your evil assemblies. Your New Moon festivals and your appointed feasts my soul hates. They have become a burden to me; I am weary of bearing them. When you spread out your hands in prayer, I will hide my eyes from you; even if you offer many prayers, I will not listen. Your hands are full of blood; wash and make yourselves clean. Take your evil deeds out of my sight! Stop doing wrong, learn to do right! Seek justice, encourage the oppressed. Defend the cause of the fatherless, plead the case of the widow. Come now, let us reason together," says the Lord. "Though your sins are like scarlet, they shall be white as snow; though they are as red as crimson, they shall be as wool."

I asked that the verse be interpreted, focusing on the word *sins* within the context of the passage. To my amazement the majority of the class wrote a traditional statement of Christian faith. Believe me I have no problem with either the Apostles' or Nicene Creeds, but Isaiah 1:1-18 in its context is not addressing personal faith. It is addressing the sins of a nation, corporate sin. I asked the class to bring another typed essay—this time interpreting Isaiah 1:1-18 *in its context.*

Many of my students exhibited in their second writing that they grasped the fact that the *sins* of Isaiah 1:1-18 are societal sins, the sins of a nation against its poor, its oppressed, its widows and its orphans. These *sins* of verse eighteen are named in the first seventeen verses. Any interpretation that focuses on transgressions not named in the chapter serves only as an excuse for inaction, refusal to stop inflicting societal pain on the unfortunate many. So often those of us who look to the Bible as a rule of faith and practice overlook its heartbeat, the suffering of the least of these. The first seventeen verses reveal the prophet's aching heart—a people who do not understand, a brood of evildoers, children given to corruption, bringers of meaningless offerings, conveners of evil assemblies, hands held up in prayer, hands full of blood, ignoring the orphan, neglecting the widow and overlooking the oppressed.

My students in their attempt to find meaning in Isaiah 1:1-18 came to a gold mine and found that gold only on their second writing, which finally followed the necessary steps for clear writing.

Step One: Choose a Topic

Now that the students finally understood Isaiah 1:1-18, they were able to choose a topic from the passage. Some of the choices were as follows:

1. Communal sin versus individual sin.
2. Special groups of people who are sinned against.
3. Hypocrisy of those who pretend to be faithful while they sin against others.
4. God's repudiation of empty offerings.
5. The opposite of sin is loving God and loving your neighbor as yourself.

Step Two: Make a List of Ideas

Making a list of ideas is brainstorming on paper. The list jump-starts the paper-writing process. Of course some early ideas will not make it to the finished paper, and of course, new ideas will surface during the preparation and writing. Your list of ideas is not meant to bind you. Creating it simply increases the chances of a clear workable outline.

Had the students who attempted the Isaiah paper started with a list of ideas similar to the list that follows, they would have discovered the richness of the passage. Scrutiny of the opening seventeen verses of the first chapter of Isaiah causes the eighteenth verse to open like a bud eager to become a flower. The list of ideas leaps from the page:

1. Isaiah's vision concerning Judah and Jerusalem
2. Oxen and donkeys know
3. Guilt ridden
4. Corrupt children
5. Turned their backs

6. Persistent rebels
7. Severe head injury
8. Whole heart afflicted
9. Wounds
10. Welts
11. Open sores
12. No bandages
13. No ointment
14. No oil
15. Burned cities
16. Stripped fields
17. Foreign intrusion
18. A city under siege
19. Like Sodom and Gomorrah
20. Rulers of Sodom
21. Multitudes of useless sacrifices
22. Excess of displeasing burnt offerings
23. Trampled courts
22. Meaningless offerings
23. Odoriferous incense
24. Convocations I cannot stand
25. Evil assemblies
26. Appointed feasts that my soul hates
27. Hands lifted in prayer that I cannot look upon
28. Many prayers that I will not hear
29. Hands full of blood
30. Evil deeds out of my sight
31. Stop doing wrong
32. Embrace righteousness
33. Learn to do right
34. Jeremiah's wounds undressed
35. Encourage the oppressed
36. Defend the cause of the fatherless
37. Plead the case of the widow
38. Seeking justice

This master of Hebrew poetry closes his long list of indictments by focusing on the imperative that righteousness and justice prevail for the downtrodden, the fatherless and the widow. From this list we see that the obvious indictment from the Lord comes against systemic sin, sins of a country and a city, sins of a society against God and her fellow citizens.

Step Three: Make Categories from the List of Ideas

I suggest that the list of ideas be written down the left side of the paper, leaving room for the ideas to be grouped to the right of the list. Grouping the ideas into categories accomplishes several things. First, it weeds out the stray ideas; fruitful brainstorming always brings some chaff along with the wheat. On the other hand, new ideas may emerge that did not appear in the original list of ideas. Here are some categories—ways to group the ideas:

1. Sick society
2. Devastated cities
3. Bloody hands
4. Come reason: encourage, defend, plead
5. Corrupt leaders
6. Rebellious children
7. False worship

Step Four: Arrange the Categories from Least Important to Most Important

The practice of arranging ideas from least to most important holds true for the essay, the thesis, the dissertation. Good preaching, good teaching and good speeches often follow this pattern. However, newspaper articles reverse this practice by placing the most important information first and the least important information last. Editorial writing in newspapers follows the rule stated in step four.

Groups of categories like lists of ideas sometimes overlap and repeat themselves, and the order of the arrangement remains in the hands of the writer. The order of the categories I see emerging from the above list is false worship, sick cities, corrupt leaders and "come, let us reason together," which is the cure. And now we are ready to create the helpful outline.

Step Five: Create a Topical Outline

When completing an assignment, use the outline style that your instructor recommends. Most professors and teachers do not require that you submit the outline with your paper, but some will require evidence that an outline was part of your preparation.

I am asking that you make a topical outline for *you*. The topical outline like the list of ideas eases the process. The outline serves the writer and therefore can remain flexible.

Thesis: Judah has deceived herself into seeking money, weapons and idols. Her errant ways have resulted in neglecting the things that could have saved her national soul.

I. Corrupt leaders
   A. "You rulers of Sodom" (Isa. 1:10)
   B. Desolate country (kings and priests) (Isa. 1:7)
   C. "Cities burned with fire" (Isa. 1:7)

II. Corrupt Followers
   A. "You people of Gomorrah" (Isa. 1:10)
   B. "Enough of your burnt offerings," your evil assemblies (Isa. 1:11)
   C. Hands full of blood (Isa. 1:15)

III. Remedy for Corruption (Isa. 1:18-20)
   A. Seek justice; practice righteousness (Isa. 1:17)
   B. "Encouraged the oppressed" (Isa. 1:17a)
   C. Defend the orphan; rescue the widow (Isa. 1:17b)
   D. Relief from sin and corruption (Isa. 1:18)

Isaiah 1:1-18 offers abundant opportunities to write about justice and righteousness. There is no denying that the sins that are *like scarlet* and *red as crimson* are national sins that the strong have perpetrated against the weak, the privileged against the oppressed, and the loud against the voiceless. A claim that alleges that Isaiah 1:18 calls only individual sinners to come to Christ to be forgiven misses the power of the passage and disregards its message. The *sins* of Isaiah 1:18 that have been enumerated clearly in the first seventeen verses are the sins of a nation that has lost touch with the heart of God. Surely, individuals need their sins forgiven; however, to emphasize individual salvation at the risk of passing over indulgently societal sins against the poor is dangerous.

Step Six: Visualize the Body of the Paper (from the Introductory Paragraph to the Conclusion of the Paper)

By *introductory* I mean the first paragraph of the essay. The following guide has been used successfully by hundreds of my students who had not yet discovered a comfortable, consistent way to begin their essays.

The All-Important First Paragraph

A clear understanding of how to begin brings a confidence that remains until the paper closes. Every paragraph wherever it appears should include a topic sentence, a beginning, a middle and an end, closely woven sentences and a closing emphatic sentence.

I teach the paragraph using the metaphor of a cluster of grapes. Most of my students understand that a bunch of grapes could never have anything growing in it but grapes—never a fig, pear, peach, banana, only grapes. The topic sentence, the first sentence of the paragraph, announces the subject matter for the entire paragraph. Therefore, no unrelated or extraneous subject matter can be included in the paragraph. My students often tell me that they feel such and such information, although unrelated, is sufficiently important to be brought into their paragraphs. I tell them that whenever they have that urge, create a new paragraph for the new idea.

When I discuss the shaping of a paragraph, I mention the happy toy that we call a Slinky. I hope everyone has watched a Slinky walk down steps. The sentences in a well-organized paragraph move down the page with the same ease that the Slinky steps down the staircase. There are no bumps, no leaps, no misses, only deliberate moves from sentence to sentence down the paragraph.

Step Seven: Conclusion of the Paper (Restates in Other Words the Thesis Statement)

A speech, presentation, sermon or essay is more effective if the least important point is presented first, and the most important point is presented last. If a writer wants most to convince his reader that the point of the Isaiah passage is a call to righteousness and justice, then everything in the paper up to the conclusion must prove that final statement.

The body of the essay contains standard, balanced paragraphs, each featuring a topic sentence that moves in an orderly fashion toward the conclusion. Sentences that relate to the topic within the paragraph help maintain the unity of the paragraph and provide linkages for the following paragraphs.

The unity of the whole essay is maintained through intentional transitions from each paragraph to the next. There are many ways to transition from paragraph to paragraph; here are a few:

1. Pick up an idea from the preceding paragraph and announce it in the first sentence of the new paragraph.

An example of (1) picking up an idea from the preceding paragraph and announcing it comes in the first paragraph of Daniel Berrigan's *Isaiah: Spirit of Courage, Gift of Tears*:

> The book of Isaiah begins with a "vision" that he "saw," not a word that he heard. But the vision is translated, transmitted, in words. **Moral** instruction that follows grows out of the vision. Such, according to the prophets, is the only **morality** worth talking about or taking seriously. The implication is inescapable; the prophet has seen the vision, the hope of God for our human kind.
>
> What might be the **moral** conduct of those who have seen and been led by a vision, who strive to care for the widow and orphan, the homeless, the refugees, and the war veterans in our midst? Such tasks require sure vision, one that is constantly renewed, a vision of God who instructs in godly behavior. (5)

The picking up of an idea from the preceding paragraph is the most frequently used of the three methods. This one comes naturally. We do this effortlessly. Moving from the introductory paragraph to the second paragraph is the pulling of a red thread in and out of a cotton bedsheet. The red thread symbolizes the unity of the essay. Therefore, the idea that is picked up to be developed must be on track. The track has been laid down beginning at the thesis statement and ending at the paper's conclusion. I would not say that any idea in any paragraph is all right to develop. I would say that any idea picked up and moving the reader on the track toward the conclusion does a good thing. The conclusion of the essay serves as an extension of the thesis statement. The thesis statement is the springboard that sends the diver toward the water. And the water represents the body of the paper. That red thread continues through the body of the paper until it takes the reader to the conclusion.

The transition is made in the first sentence of the new paragraph and may or may not be the exact words used in the previous paragraph. You will have fun searching the paragraph for key ideas that will move your essay in the desired direction. I have read dozens of compositions, seat-of-the-pants efforts that went awry by jumping ship early. These student writers jumped ship by pulling from thin air the ideas for their paragraphs rather than picking up and developing ideas from the preceding paragraph.

2. Repeat a word in the first sentence of the new paragraph from the last sentence of the preceding paragraph.

From Walter Brueggemann's *Isaiah 1-39* comes an example of repeating a word in the first sentence of the new paragraph taken from the last sentence of the preceding paragraph.

> For that reason we are not quite prepared for verses 16-17, which suggest that there is yet a route back to Yahweh. We will see this inclination often in the book of Isaiah. This particular prophetic tradition is as honest and as harsh as the traditions of Jeremiah and Ezekiel. But it is much more reluctant than they to anticipate the complete nullification of Israel. The book of Isaiah endlessly seeks, against the terrible consequences Judah deserved, to keep a **hope** alive for this people of God.

The **hope** offered here is a series of nine imperatives suggesting that Israel can be restored to Yahweh, but only with profound, intentional changes. The actions required are not the ones dismissed in verses 10-15, but are more elemental. It is as though the poet says, for Yahweh, 'Don't talk of love, show me!' The actions urged, if Judah is to have a chance, are of two kinds. First, in the center of the urging (v.16b) are three general statements about evil and good. That seems too obvious, except that Israel had lost its way even on such elemental categories (5:20). Restored relationship with Yahweh requires good in the place of evil. Israel must engage in ritual purification because it has been defiled and made unacceptable to the holy God (v.16). The "washing" here to be done is the same as that which David offers in Psalm 51:2, only here it is Israel who must wash, that is, the whole people. We will see in 6:5 that the prophet is not indifferent to ritual cleansing. Life with Yahweh must be undefiled, and the community must use the available means to become ritually acceptable (18).

Repeating a word from the last sentence of the preceding paragraph serves two purposes. First, this procedure forces the writer to take care of the words used in the last sentence of each paragraph. Some writing teachers point out that the first sentence of each paragraph is the topic sentence while the last sentence of the paragraph is the emphatic sentence. The last sentence of the paragraph often will be the sentence with the most punch and will launch the writer and reader into the content of the next paragraph. The literal repeating of a word from the last sentence of the previous paragraph works well at this point. Second, this procedure makes the transition. And the repeated word can be written anywhere in the first sentence of the new paragraph. One of the joys that I have experienced from having taught so many years in the college classroom is recalling the responses, or I should say the gentle protests, from students to certain assertions made by the professor. For years I have taught that repeating a word from the last sentence of the preceding paragraph maintains unity. I have done this a hundred times. And I tell you that most of those times at least one scholar said something to this effect, "I was taught never to repeat such and such, and Ms. So-and-So said that was needless repetition." It never fails; there's one in almost every class. And that's all right because it helps clear the air. I'm sure that Ms. So-and-So said something about not repeating oneself needlessly. She was right. But she was not addressing how to make transitions from one paragraph to the next.

3. Begin the sentence of the new paragraph with a transitional word; both conjunctive adverbs and some coordinate conjunctions work nicely as transitional words. Some conjunctive adverbs are *therefore, thus, nonetheless, however, consequently, furthermore*; some of the coordinate conjunctions are *and, for, but*.

An example of using a transitional word between paragraphs comes again from Daniel Berrigan's *Isaiah: Spirit of Courage, Gift of Tears*:

> The advantage in the present, according to Isaiah, inevitably belongs to the powerful. The wicked have in their favor, tactically speaking, the refusal of the faithful to use their methods. The wicked then cannot summon the excuse that they are only "responding in kind." Nothing of the tactic they have used on others has been their own fate; they act in a kind of void of malevolence. They exercise evil, killing, control, for the pure hell of it; which is to say, for the ego of it.
>
> **Nevertheless**, judgment is inescapable. It is in the nature of God, who is a God of justice. God in justice (holiness) created and so endowed us with God's own passion for "fair play, fair share" access to power, protection, and vindication in the human drama (81).

Using transitional words such as conjunctive adverbs and coordinate conjunctions makes crisp transitions from one paragraph to the next. Conjunctive adverbs like *therefore, however* and *furthermore* within themselves reach back into what has been written in the previous paragraph and point ahead to what will be said in the new paragraph.

Coordinate conjunctions like *and, but* and *yet* do the same thing. Like the Roman household god, Janus, they look backward and forward at the same time.

We consult St. Paul on theological questions; let us take a peek at one of his transitions from paragraph to paragraph. This New Testament giant concludes one paragraph at the close of the seventh chapter of Romans and begins a new paragraph in the first verse of the eighth chapter. Look please at how he does this. Romans 7:25b reads,

> So then, I myself in my mind am a slave to God's law, but in the sinful nature a slave to the law of sin.

This verse ends the last paragraph and chapter 7. The new chapter and new paragraph begin with "**Therefore,** there is now no condemnation for those who are in Christ Jesus." Please note that here and in many other places St. Paul's sentences move from paragraph to paragraph using conjunctive adverbs and coordinate conjunctions.

Each method listed above has proven to be a foolproof way to attain unity throughout the essay. A look at each of the three ways to move from one paragraph to the next will show the writer the way to make smooth transitions. The length of the conclusion is to be determined by the writer of the essay. I have read splendid conclusions that were full, well-developed paragraphs. I have read conclusions that were no longer than a few sentences at the end of the final paragraph. More important than the length of the conclusion is what it does. It's the icing on the cake. Sheridan Baker calls it the home punch. It brings closure. It seals. It punctuates. It speaks the last Amen. It says again in words not used in the thesis statement what the thesis statement has stated. It says what the writer burns to say. It invites the reader to buy the product. It closes the deal. It makes the hand shake that seals the transaction. It ends with a bang and not with a whimper.

Self-Quiz for Chapter Eleven: Writing That Paper

1. What in the mind of the student rescued Dr. Beaty from being a dull English professor?
2. Exodus 17:14a teaches what about remembering?
3. Exodus 34:1 tells what happened to the first writing of the Ten Commandments. What happened to the first copy?
4. What necessitated the writing of the book of Deuteronomy?

5. What talent do we know was possessed by at least one of the spies sent in to survey the promise land?
6. What is the strange metaphor of Psalm 45:1?
7. The teachers of the law and the Pharisees wanted to stone the adulterous woman in John 8. What did Rabbi Jesus want to do with her?
8. What group of people in John 8 first dropped their stones and left the Temple courts?
9. What might Rabbi Jesus have written on the ground at the scene of arresting the woman?
10. Often the message of the metaphor is stronger than what?
11. What are the first two items on our "to do" list in writing the essay?
12. Dr. Beaty received a paper on rap music; what did he do first?
13. What did Dr. Beaty do after he read the paper on rap music?
14. The students who botched the Isaiah writing assignment should have started with what?
15. State the main difference between the Isaiah students who failed and the Richard Petty student who succeeded.
16. This chapter mentions three different kinds of outlines; name them.
17. Of the three outlines mentioned in this chapter, *Sacred Grammar* recommends which one for our purposes?
18. What is the significance of the metaphor, the cluster of grapes?
19. Sheridan Baker and *Sacred Grammar* ask that the thesis statement appear where in the essay?
20. Define concrete image.
21. Of the three ways to make transitions from paragraph to paragraph, which one is used most frequently?
22. What two groups of transitional words work well as the first word in a new paragraph?
23. How does the motion of the Slinky help the writer improve paragraphs?
24. Sheridan Baker's opening invitation does what?
25. Paul the Apostle used what transitional word to begin the eighth chapter of Romans?
26. Who determines the length of the conclusion of a given essay?

EPILOGUE

I've seen these methods help countless students move from confusion to clarity in their writing. Some, who seemed hopelessly lost trying to express themselves with the written word, used the methods in *Sacred Grammar* to find their way to clear, energetic writing. People from grade school to graduate school have used these instructions and transformed their ability to write from dread to confidence. The second best thing to my being with you to guide you is having a copy of this book open beside you as you write.

James Wilson Beaty, PhD

Jeremiah 22:16

Atlanta

2010

APPENDIX

Self-Quiz for Chapter One: The Eight Parts of Speech

1. Define a clause.
   A clause is a group of related words that contains a subject and a verb.
2. Define a phrase.
   A phrase is a group of related words that does not contain a subject and a verb.
3. Define a predicate.
   A predicate is a verb and all the words that follow it in its clause.
4. What determines a word's part of speech in a sentence?
   A word's function or use in a sentence determines its part of speech.
5. Define a simple sentence.
   A simple sentence contains only one independent clause.
6. Sir Winston Churchill said what about the preposition?
   Understanding the preposition leads to an understanding of the sentence.
7. List seven coordinate conjunctions.
   For, and, nor, but, or, yet, so
8. List ten subordinate conjunctions.
   After, although, because, before, even though, if, since, until, when, while
9. List ten prepositions.
   At, by, concerning, during, in, like, of, on, over, to, under
10. Define a preposition.
    A preposition is a word that joins its object to the rest of the sentence.

11. Name the most frequently used type of phrase in English.
    The prepositional phrase
12. What is the most frequent comma splice error?
    The comma placed between two independent clauses
13. Write the eight parts of speech.
    Noun, pronoun, verb, adjective, adverb, conjunction, preposition, interjection
14. Define a noun.
    A noun is a word that names a person, place or thing.
15. Define a pronoun.
    A pronoun is a word that takes the place of a noun.
16. Define a verb.
    A verb is a word that expresses action or a state of being.
17. Define an adjective.
    An adjective is a word that describes a noun or a pronoun.
18. Define an adverb.
    An adverb describes verbs, adjectives and other adverbs.
19. Define a conjunction.
    A conjunction joins words or groups of words.
20. Define a preposition.
    A preposition joins its object to the rest of the sentence.
21. Define an interjection.
    An interjection is a word or group of words that exclaims.
22. Explain the vertical and horizontal approaches to the eight parts of speech.
    The vertical approach learns the definition only while the horizontal approach understands the relationships of the parts of speech within the sentence.
23. What is the cardinal rule about subject-verb agreement that will never change?
    The subject of the sentence and its verb will always agree in number.
24. Adverbs describe what parts of speech?
    Verbs, adjectives and other adverbs
25. Adjectives describe what parts of speech?
    Nouns and pronouns
26. How is a collegiate dictionary especially helpful in the study of grammar?
    Gives all possible parts of speech.

27. Flash cards serve what purpose in the study of grammar in this text, *Sacred Grammar*?
    Review and memorization

Written exercises for Chapter One: The Eight Parts of Speech

1. Write five simple sentences. Underline each subject with one line and each verb with two lines.
2. Write a brief paragraph explaining the vertical and horizontal approaches to learning the eight parts of speech. In each sentence underline each subject with one line and each complete verb with two lines. Place [brackets] around each complete clause. Note: This begins our decorating sentences, which we will look at in a later chapter.

Self-Quiz for Chapter Two: The Case for the Three Cases

1. Name the three cases in English.
   Subjective, objective, possessive
2. What two parts of speech have case?
   Nouns and pronouns
3. How many of the remaining six parts of speech have case?
   Not one
4. A noun or pronoun following a preposition (in a prepositional phrase) is written in what case?
   Objective case
5. The part of a sentence before (in front of) a verb is called what "territory"?
   The subject territory
6. The part of a sentence following (after) a verb is called what "territory?
   The object territory
7. The pronouns *I, he, she, they, we, who* are always what case?
   Subjective
8. The pronouns *me, them, us, him, whom* are always what case?
   Objective
9. The pronouns *his, hers, our, their, whose* are always what case?
   Possessive
10. List seven relative pronouns.

That, who, whom, whose, which, what, whatever
11. What do relative pronouns introduce?
    Dependent clauses
12. What do relative pronouns do to the clause that follows them?
    Make them dependent
13. Why is the singular possessive case of Jesus and Moses written with the apostrophe (') immediately following the second *s*?
    Jesus' and Moses' already contain the second s sound

Writing Exercise for Chapter Two: The Case for the Three Cases

1. Write ten pronouns.
   I, you, he, she, it, we, they, them, us
2. Make 3 × 5 flashcards.
3. Write seven relative pronouns.
   That, who, whom, which, whose, what, whatever
4. Write five sentences whose relative pronouns introduce relative, subordinate clauses.
5. Each noun and pronoun is one of three cases whenever they appear in a sentence. Name those three cases.
   Subjective, objective and possessive

Self-quiz for Chapter Three: The Simple Sentence

1. Define a clause.
   A clause is a group of related words that contains a subject and a verb.
2. Name the two kinds of clauses.
   Independent and dependent
3. In our system what is a changing word?
   A subordinate conjunction or a relative pronoun that changes an independent clause to a dependent clause.
4. The two groups of changing words are called what?
   Subordinate conjunctions and relative pronouns
5. What is the shortest verse in the Bible? What does it say?
   John 11:35 says, "Jesus wept."
6. What is a fragment?

A fragment is a group of words that contains a subject and verb and has been made a dependent clause by the presence of a subordinate conjunction or a relative pronoun

7. How are fragments like walks or bases on balls in the great game of baseball? Intentional walks in baseball serve a good purpose hoping to gain an out with the next batter. Intentional fragments serve good purposes placed among sentences. However, the unintentional fragment like the unintentional base on balls must be avoided.
8. Why is "Jesus wept" a sentence?
It is an independent clause.
9. Why is "Then Jesus wept" a sentence?
"Then Jesus wept" has a subject and verb that has not been made dependent by the adverb *then*.
10. Why is "When Jesus wept" not a sentence?
It's a fragment that has been made dependent with the presence of the subordinate conjunction *when*.
11. What is the one requirement in order to have a sentence?
One independent clause
12. What kind of clause does a simple sentence never have?
Dependent
13. Can a simple sentence have two subjects and two verbs?
Yes, these are called compound subjects and compound verbs, not a compound sentence.
14. In Jeremiah 5:11 what part of speech is the word *unfaithful*?
Adjective
15. Every verb denoted either _____ or _____.
Action or state of being
16. Are the two verbs in Amos 5:11a action or state of being verbs?
Both are action verbs
17. What is the importance of the acronym FANBOYS?
Helps remember the seven coordinate conjunctions
18. Write the seven coordinate conjunctions.
For, and, nor, but, or, yet, so
19. When is the word *after* a preposition?
When it forms a prepositional phrase and joins its object to the rest on the sentence. He lives *in a house in the mountains.*
20. When is the word *after* a subordinate conjunction?

When it subordinates a clause and makes it dependent. *After* Jesus wept over the sins of Jerusalem, he fasted.
21. What do Harold Bloom, Martin Luther King and E. B. White have in common? All three begin sentences with *and* and *but*.
22. The word *however* is a conjunctive adverb. Does it ever make the clause following it dependent?
No
23. List five conjunctive adverbs.
However, therefore, nonetheless, thus, consequently, furthermore
24. List five subordinate conjunctions.
Although, because, if, since, when, while
25. Who won the 2010 World Series?

Self-Quiz Chapter Four: The Complex Sentence

1. Define the simple sentence.
A simple sentence contains only one independent clause.
2. Define the complex sentence.
A complex sentence contains only one independent clause and one or more dependent clauses.
3. Define subordination.
Subordination is changing an independent clause into a dependent clause using either a subordinate conjunction or a relative pronoun.
4. What is meant in this lesson by changing word?
The changing word changes the independent clause to a dependent clause using either a subordinate conjunction or a relative pronoun.
5. What is the first complex sentence in the Gospel of Mark?
Mark 1:10, "As Jesus was coming up out of the water, he saw heaven being torn open and the Spirit descending on him like a dove."
6. Name the two categories of words that are the changing words.
Subordinate conjunctions and relative pronouns.
7. The New Testament was written originally in what language?
Greek
8. Write an example of a subject-verb cluster and what does it form?
Jesus wept forms an independent clause.
9. What is a sentence fragment?

The most common sentence fragment is the dependent clause posing as a sentence. *While Jesus wept.*
10. List ten subordinate conjunctions. Be sure to include three that have more than one word. As soon as, even though, as, after, before, although, ever since
11. List seven relative pronouns.
    That, who, whom, whose, which, what, whatever
12. List two coordinate conjunctions that may be used to begin sentences.
    And, but
13. How do complex sentences create a "flow" from paragraph to paragraph?
    Dependent clauses at the beginning of sentences that begin with subordinate conjunctions flow as water flows over rocks in a mountain stream.
14. What two groups of words give evidence of subordination?
    Subordinate conjunctions and relative pronouns
15. What are three additional names for the dependent clause?
    Subordinate clause, introductory clause, adverbial clause
16. What is the name of words that come from verbs, look like verbs and have every indication of being verbs but are not verbs?
    Verbals
17. In order to determine if a clause is independent or dependent, we ask what three questions for our clause test?
    Is there a verb? Does that verb have a subject forming a subject-verb cluster? Does the cluster have in front of it a changing word subordinator, a subordinate conjunction or a relative pronoun?
18. Name the three cases in English.
    Subjective, objective, possessive
19. Explain the three steps necessary to form the plural possessive case form of nouns.
    (1) Make the noun plural; (2) check to see if the plural form of the word ends with the letter *s*; and (3) if it ends with the letter *s*, the apostrophe follows immediately the letter *s*. Note: If the word does not end with the letter *s* or an *s* sound, the plural word is punctuated with the apostrophe as though the word were singular possessive. For example, Men's Conference
20. Name the talented and brilliant manager of the Atlanta Braves Baseball Club. He retired in 2010

Bobby Cox

Self-Quiz Chapter Five: The Compound Sentence

1. Define a compound sentence.
   A compound sentence contains two or more dependent clauses.
2. Define subordination.
   Subordination is the changing of an independent clause to a dependent clause using a subordinate conjunction or a relative pronoun.
3. What two parts of speech subordinate clauses?
   Subordinate clauses and relative pronouns
4. Why do compound sentences contain no subordinators?
   Compound sentences do not contain dependent clauses ever, thus, no subordinate conjunctions or relative pronouns.
5. Name the fours ways of separating independent clauses in a compound sentence.
   This chapter speaks of the four ways: (1) Jesus wept, but the disciples slept; (2) Jesus wept; the disciples slept, (3) Jesus wept; however, the disciples slept; (4) Jesus wept: Jerusalem broke his heart. Note: Number 4 above is the least frequently used way to punctuate between independent clauses. As stated in this chapter, the colon (:) works instead of the semicolon (;) whenever the content of the second clause is closely connected to the content of the clause immediately before it.
6. What is the significance of the acronym FANBOYS?
   An acronym helps to jumpstart the memory. Each letter in FANBOYS stands for one of the seven coordinate conjunctions: for, and, nor, but, or, yet, so.
7. State the comma rule that applies to coordinate conjunctions.
   The rule states, "Place a comma before (in front of) a coordinate conjunction when it joins two independent clauses."
8. What is the most frequently used punctuation between two independent clauses?
   The comma rule stated just above in number 7; the comma before the coordinate conjunction.
9. What is the least used punctuation between independent clauses?
   The colon (:)

10. The semicolon (;) between independent clauses resembles what mark in a mathematical equation?
    The equal sign (=)
11. Is the compound sentence limited to the number of independent clauses it may have?
    No
12. What is the most frequent comma usage error?
    The comma splice, placing a comma between two independent clauses
13. Why do many writers avoid using the semicolon?
    They are unsure that it is an equal sign separating structurally equal elements in the sentence
14. In this lesson what Hebrew prophet is likened to American poet Walt Whitman?
    Jeremiah
15. The first two ways mentioned in this chapter to punctuate between independent clauses are (, and) and the semicolon (;). What part of speech is used to implement the third choice of punctuation mentioned in this chapter?
    The conjunctive adverb
16. Sameness of sentence structure brings what result?
    Boredom, ennui
17. Write the comma rule that addresses introductory clauses or phrases.
    "Place a comma after a long introductory clause of phrase." Note: most teachers of writing and some grammar texts feel that "long" means six or more words.
18. Do subordinate conjunctions ever subordinate clauses?
    Never
19. Can a conjunctive adverb ever be a changing word subordinator?
    Never
20. List twenty (20) subordinate conjunctions.
    after, although, as if, as though, because, before, even if, even though, how, if, in case, in that, insofar as, no matter how, now that, once, provided (that), since, so that, than, though, unless, until, when, whenever, where, wherever, whether, while (*Hodges' Harbrace Handbook,* fifteenth edition, page 41)
21. List twenty (20) conjunctive adverbs.

also, anyhow, anyway, besides, consequently, finally, furthermore, hence, however, incidentally, indeed, instead, likewise, meanwhile, moreover, nevertheless, nonetheless, next, otherwise, similarly, still, then, therefore, thus (*Hodges' Harbrace Handbook,* fifteenth edition, page 68).

22. List seven (7) relative pronouns.
    that, who, whom, whose, which, what, whatever
23. Can the words *after* and *before* function as different parts of speech?
    Yes
24. When are *after* and *before* subordinate conjunctions?
    Whenever *after* and *before* are written before (in front of) an independent clause that clause changes to a dependent clause and both *after* and *before* become subordinate conjunctions (changing words).
25. List five (5) coordinate conjunctions.
    for, and, nor, but, or, yet, so

Self-Quiz for Chapter Six: The Compound-Complex Sentence

1. Name the four kinds of sentences according to structure.
   Simple, complex, compound, compound-complex
2. In this text, *Sacred Grammar,* what precisely do we mean by "structure"?
   Structure means how the sentence is built; the number and kinds of clauses determine a sentence's structure.
3. Define a clause.
   A clause is a group of related words that contains a subject and a verb
4. What are the names of the two primary segments or groups of words that we use in this grammar text?
   Clauses and phrases
5. Define a simple sentence.
   A simple sentence contains only one independent clause.
6. Define a complex sentence.
   A complex sentence contains only one independent clause and one or more dependent clauses
7. Define a compound sentence.
   A compound sentence contains two or more independent clauses.

8. Define a compound-complex sentence.
   A compound-complex sentence contains two or more independent clauses and one or more dependent clauses.
9. Why do expressions such as "a complete thought" and "convey an idea" fail to define a sentence?
   Neither complete thoughts nor ideas conveyed necessarily form sentences. Neither "Ouch!" nor "Glory to God!" is a sentence. But both convey ideas.
10. Identify the dependent clause in Jeremiah 3:7.
    after she had done all this
11. Name the subordinator (subordinate conjunction or relative pronoun) in Jeremiah 3:7. after
12. Define a fragment.
    A fragment is a group of words that is not an independent clause, either a phrase or a dependent clause that sometimes poses incorrectly as a sentence. Note: Some fragments like intentional bases on balls are useful.
13. Why is it a good practice to learn the definitions of sentences in the following order: simple, complex, compound, compound-complex?
    One (simple) and two (complex) are sequential. "Only one independent clause . . . only one independent clause and one or more . . ."
14. Write a simple sentence.
    Jesus wept in the garden.
15. Write a complex sentence.
    Jesus wept in the garden while the disciples slept.
16. Write a compound sentence.
    Jesus wept in the garden; the disciples slept in the barn.
17. Write a compound-complex sentence.
    Jesus wept; the disciples slept while the multitudes ate loaves and fishes.
18. List fifteen (15) subordinate conjunctions.
    after, although, because, before, even though, how, if, once, provided (that), since, so that, though, unless
19. List seven (7) relative pronouns.
    that, who, whom, which, whose, what, whatever
20. What three steps are helpful to determine whether a clause is dependent or independent?

The clause test asks three questions: (1) Is a verb present? (2) Does that verb have a subject? (3) Is a subordinator (subordinate conjunction or relative pronoun) present in front of the verb. If no subordinator is present, the clause is independent. If a subordinator is present (changing word), the clause has been made dependent by subordination.

21. What marks are written beneath subjects and verbs?
    One straight line beneath the subject, and two straight lines beneath the verb.

Self-Quiz for Chapter Seven: Decorating Sentences

1. How is decorating sentences different from diagramming them?
   In decorating the words remain written across the page and are marked accordingly. Subjects, verb, direct objects are underlined; complements are circled with an oval and complete clauses are enclosed within brackets, etc., etc. Diagramming works down the paper under the written sentence.
2. How many marks are used to decorate sentences?
   Eight
3. Write all those eight marks and write beside them which each one indicates.
   One line under the subject of the verb, two straight lines under the complete verb, four straight lines under the indirect object, three straight lines under the direct object, the circle (oval) around subordinators, (parentheses) around phrases, and [brackets] around complete clauses.
4. How do we decorate "Jesus wept"?
   One straight line under *Jesus*, two straight lines under *wept*, [brackets] around the complete clause
5. Is "Jesus wept" a clause and if so what kind? Explain.
   "Jesus wept" is an independent clause because it contains a verb and a subject with no subordinator present.
6. What mark in decorating sentences indicates phrases?
   (parentheses)
7. What mark in decorating sentences indicates clauses?
   [brackets]
8. What three steps are taken in what we call the clause test?

(1) Is there is verb present? (2) Is there a subject of that verb present? (3) Does that subject-verb clause cluster have a subordinator that makes the clause dependent?
9. Name the two groups of words that change independent clauses to dependent clauses?
Subordinate clauses and relative pronouns
10. The acronym FANBOYS stands for what group of words? Name the seven words. Coordinate conjunctions: for, and, nor, but, or, yet, so
11. Do good writers begin sentences with coordinate conjunctions such as *and* and *but*?
Yes
12. Name four great writers who begin sentences with *and* and *but*.
Harold Bloom, Martin Luther King, Jr., William Shakespeare and E. B. White
13. Name the three verbals.
Gerunds, infinitives and participles
14. Explain the difference between a direct object and a complement.
A direct object is a noun or pronoun that follows a transitive, action verb; the direct object receives the action of the action verb; a pronoun that is a direct object is always written in the objective case. A complement, however, is a noun or pronoun that follows a linking verb, often some form of the verb *to be*. Example of a direct object: God loves homeless *people*. The word *people* receives the action of the verb loves. Example of a complement: Homeless people are *citizens* too. The word *citizens* is a predicate noun complement that renames the subject *people*.
15. A complement can be what three parts of speech? Noun, pronoun or adjective
16. What kinds of verbs have direct objects following them? action verbs and transitive verbs
17. What kinds of verbs have complements following them? linking and intransitive
18. Define predicate. A predicate is the verb of the sentence and all the words that follow it in its clause
19. A predicate noun renames what? the subject of the verb
20. A predicate adjective describes what? the subject of the verb

21. A predicate noun renames what?
    The subject
22. A predicate adjective describes what?
    The subject

Self-Quiz for Chapter Eight: Verbs, Nouns' Best Friends

1. What does Patricia O'Connor say that verbs do for nouns?
   Verbs keep nouns from standing around with their hands in their pockets.
2. Verbs possess two talents; name them.
   They express action and they show state of being
3. Name and define the eight parts of speech.
   (1) Noun, a person, place or thing; (2) pronoun, a word that takes the place of a noun; (3) verb, a word that expresses action or a state of being; (4) adjective, a word that describes a noun or a pronoun; (5) adverb, a word that describes a verb, an adjective or another adverb; (6) conjunction, a word or group of words that joins words or groups of words; (7) preposition, a word that joins its object to the rest of the sentence; and (8) interjection, a word that exclaims
4. Define a clause.
   A clause is a group of related words that contains a subject and a verb
5. When a verb is transitive, what follows it?
   A direct object
6. Where do we look first to find the part of speech of a particular word?
   The dictionary
7. What is the antecedent of a pronoun?
   The antecedent of a pronoun is a noun or a pronoun to which it refers earlier in its sentence or paragraph. Every pronoun must have an antecedent.
8. A pronoun must agree in number with its antecedent. Here *number* means what?
   Number refers to whether a word is singular or plural.
9. Some grammar texts name a fourth principal part of the verb. Name that fourth principal part.

The letter *s* form of the verb, She *sings*. He *preaches*. It *flies*, i.e., the need to place the letter *s* on the third person singular form of every single verb in the regular present tense.
10. The *s* form appears in what tense, what person and what number of the verb?
    Regular present tense, third person singular
11. What is one cardinal grammar rule that will remain?
    The subject and verb will always agree in number—singular verb, singular subject; plural verb, plural subject.
12. If a verb has a direct object, what do we call that verb?
    A transitive verb
13. There are two broad categories of verbs. One category is the action verb. The second is what?
    Linking or intransitive verb
14. The subject of the verb must be one of two parts of speech. Name the two.
    Noun or pronoun
15. What is the function of the subject of an action verb?
    The subject of the action verb names who or what is doing the acting.
16. What is the function of the subject of the state of being verb?
    The subject of the state of being verb shows who or what is in the state of being. Example: *I am. God is love.*
17. A direct object answers what question?
    The direct object answers the question, what receives the action of the action verb?
18. Only nouns and pronouns serve as subjects of verbs. Every pronoun written in English must have what?
    An antecedent
19. Write the pronoun that can refer to one person (singular) or to many people (plural).
    You
20. Verbs originate from their stems or roots. This is often called the infinitive. What are the second and third principal parts of the four verb stems of Exodus 19:4
    to go, to call, to want, to come? (went, gone) (called, called) (wanted, wanted) (came, come)

21. What is the figure of speech, metaphor or simile, found in Exodus 19:4?
"I carried you as on eagle's wings and brought you unto myself."
22. Some grammar texts refer to only three principal parts of the verb. What does this text, *Sacred Grammar,* name the three columns?
Present stem, past tense and past participle
23. What makes a verb a regular verb?
If both the past tense and the past participle are formed by adding the letter d or the letters ed, the verb is a regular verb.
24. What makes a verb an irregular verb?
If both the past tense and the past participle are NOT formed by adding the letter d or the letters ed, the verb is irregular.
25. Which verbs in which tense in English always end with the letter *s?*
regular present tense, third person singular
26. Number 11 in this quiz asks a question that I want to ask again. What one cardinal rule of grammar will never change? The subject and verb must agree in number.
27. What is a compound subject?
Two subjects of the same verb: Jack and Jill ran.
28. Name the verb, its subject, the tense of the verb, the person of the noun subject, the number of the noun subject and the number of the verb in the following dependent clause taken from 1 Kings 17:1a:. "As the Lord lives."
The verb is *lives.* The subject of the verb is *Lord.* The tense is present. The person of the subject is third person singular. The number of the subject and verb are both singular.
29. What is the error in the following sentence: "She sing in the choir."
The error is subject-verb agreement. *Sing* is plural and does not agree in number with the singular subject *she.*
30. What are the second and third principal parts of the verb stem (infinitive) to lie, meaning to rest or recline?
lay, lain
31. What are the second and third principal parts of the verb stem (infinitive) to lie, meaning to falsify, to bear false witness?
lied, lied
32. What are the second and third principal parts of the verb stem (infinitive) to lay, meaning to put or to place?

laid, laid
33. What are the second and third principal parts of the verb stem (infinitive) to shine, meaning to glow, to radiate?
shone, shone
34. What are the second and third principal parts of the verb stem (infinitive) to shine, meaning to polish?
shined, shined
35. What are the second and third principal parts of the verb stem (infinitive) to shrink? shrank, shrunk
36. Why is the verb to do (principal parts: do, did, done) an irregular verb?
Because the second and third principal parts do not end with the letters *ed*.
37. Why is the verb *to see* (principal parts: see, saw, seen) an irregular verb?
Because the second and third principal parts do not end with the letter *d* or the letters *ed*.
38. Why is the verb *to love* (principal parts: love, loved, loved) a regular verb?
Because the second and third principal parts end with the letters *ed*
39. Why is the verb *to set* (principal parts: set, set, set) an irregular verb?
Because the second and third principal parts do not end with the letter *d* or the letters *ed*
40. Name the helping (auxiliary) verbs for the present perfect tense.
has, have
41. Name the helping verb for the past perfect tense.
had
42. What verb tense is formed using the second principal part?
The past tense
43. What verb tenses are formed using the third principal part?
present perfect, past perfect, future perfect
44. Explain the time being described when using the present perfect tense.
The present perfect tense denotes continuing action in past time. Example: She has visited the dentist four times this year.
45. Explain the time being described when using the past perfect tense.

The past perfect tense refers to an action completed at a time in the past prior to another past time or past action. Example: She had finished lunch before I arrived.

46. Define a preposition.
    A preposition is a word that joins its object to the rest of the sentence forming a prepositional phrase.
47. Name the three cases in English.
    subjective case, objective case, possessive case
48. What two parts of speech have case?
    nouns and pronouns
49. Every noun written in English in the possessive case contains what mark of punctuation? An apostrophe
50. Explain the case error in the following sentence: I am him.
    The pronoun *him* is the objective form and the intransitive linking verb *am* never has an objective case form following it. Therefore the sentence should read, "I am he."
51. Explain why "I am he" is correct.
    A noun or pronoun that follows the intransitive linking verb *am* must be in the subjective case form. The pronoun *he* is the correct subjective case form.
52. Isaiah 49:16a (New Living Translation) reads, "See, I have written your name on my hand." What is the tense of that verb from Isaiah?
    The present perfect tense
53. What tense is indicated by the auxiliary helping verbs *have* and *has*?
    The present perfect tense
54. Tense conveys what?
    Tense indicates when and for how long an action or state occurs. (*Hodges' Harbrace Handbook*, p. 794)
55. What is the function of a modal auxiliary verb?
    The modal auxiliary expresses mood. An auxiliary verb that is used with another verb to indicate its mood, as *can, could, may, might, must, shall, should, will* and *would*
56. Name the three perfect tenses.
    present perfect, past perfect, future perfect
57. Name the tenses in the following sentence: Dr. Chang *will have delivered* five thousand babies by the time she *has retired*.
    The future perfect tense and the present perfect tense

58. Define mood.
    A characteristic of verbs that indicates the speaker's attitude toward the action expressed: indicative mood (a fact expressed); subjunctive mood (as a matter of supposition, contrary to fact, desire, possibility); or the imperative mood (as a command).
59. Name the three moods in English.
    indicative, subjunctive, imperative
60. Which of the three moods often omits using a subject of a verb?
    Imperative
61. The verb form has no change in what two moods?
    indicative and imperative
62. List some words or groups of words that indicate the verb to follow is in the subjunctive mood. as if, as though, if I were, I wish
63. A verb written in the indicative mood generally does what?
    states a fact
64. A verb written in the imperative mood generally does what?
    gives a command
65. Most verbs (the overwhelming majority) are written in what mood?
    indicative
66. The voice of a verb determines what about a subject?
    If the subject is doing the acting or is being acted upon
67. Name the two voices of verbs in English.
    the active voice and the passive voice
68. Which of the two voices is to be used sparingly?
    the passive voice
69. Which verb in 1 John 4:17a employs the passive voice: "In this way, love is made complete among us so that we will have confidence in the day of judgment"?
    Love is made complete among us.
70. Name the traditional six tenses in English.
    present, past, future, present perfect, past perfect, future perfect

Self-Quiz for Chapter Nine: A Moment with Verbals

1. How are the Constitution of the United States and the acquaintance with English grammar related?
   So very few people know very much of either one.
2. How do computers respond to the word *verbals*?

They underline it probably believing that it is a misspelling of the word *verb*.
3. According to Patricia O'Conner, verbs do what for nouns?
They keep them from standing around with their hands in their pockets.
4. Name the three verbals.
Gerunds, participles, infinitives
5. Verbals get their life from what?
verbs
6. Name the three principal parts of a verb.
The present tense stem (infinitive), the past tense form and the past participle. Example: break, broke, broken love, loved, loved
7. A gerund always ends with what three letters of the alphabet?
ing
8. A gerund functions as what part of speech?
noun
9. A noun or pronoun that directly precedes a gerund must be written in which of the three cases?
the possessive case
10. Give an example from scripture when a gerund is a noun, direct object of a verb. Jeremiah 7:18b, "They pour out offerings." The word *offerings* is the direct object of the verb, *pour*. The gerund *offerings* is the noun object and gets its life from the verb stem, *to offer*.
11. What is the difference in the direct object of a verb and a predicate noun?
The direct object receives the action of the verb while the predicate noun renames the subject.
12. Name the three principal parts of the verb stem *to groan*.
Groan, groaned, groaned
13. Is *to groan* a regular or irregular verb?
Regular
14. In a sentence a participle can be one of two parts of speech. Name them. adjective or adverb
15. Why is the word *deadly* in Deuteronomy 32:24 an adjective?
It describes the noun *plague*
16. Why is the word *deadly* not a participle?

A participle is a verbal. A verbal exists only with life from a verb. The word *deadly* is an adjective that does not come from any verb stem.

17. We speak of creating verbals. Explain how this happens.
    Verbals are created from verb stems. *Seeing* is *believing*. Both *Seeing* and *believing* are noun gerunds ending with the letters *ing*. *Seeing* is the noun subject of the verb *is*. It is created from the verb stem *to see*. The predicate noun *believing* is also a gerund that is created from the verb stem *to believe*. The two remaining verbals are participles and infinitives, all of which come out of verbs.
18. What determines the part of speech of a word in a sentence?
    Its function, what it does. If it's the subject of a verb it has to be a noun or a pronoun. If is shows action or state of being it has to be a verb. If it describes words it's an adjective or an adverb. Words that join words and groups of words are either conjunctions or prepositions. The eighth part of speech exclaims; it's the interjection.
19. Phrases like individual words have parts of speech. A phrase that modifies a noun or pronoun is what part of speech?
    It's an adjective phrase.
20. A phrase that modifies a verb, adverb or adjective is what part of speech?
    It's an adverbial (adverb) phrase.
21. Isaiah 1:5b contains two participles. Name the two words and tell why they are participles.
    Injured and *afflicted*, both are adjectives describing the nouns *head* and *heart*. Their verb sources are *to injure* and *to afflict*.
22. Isaiah 1:6b contains the words *cleansed, bandaged* and *soothed*. Are these words verbals? What is their part of speech?
    They are participles (adjectives) that modify the noun sores.
23. What little word indicates or announces an infinitive?
    (to) be
24. An infinitive forms which of the three principal parts of the verb?
    The first principal part or the present tense stem
25. An infinitive can function as any one of three parts of speech.
    noun, adjective or adverb
26. Verbals in good writing increase what and add what?
    They increase vocabulary and add spice.

Self-Quiz for Chapter Ten: The Comma

1. What punctuation mark gives most trouble?
   The comma
2. What may very well be the most serious punctuation error?
   The comma splice
3. What comma rule is the most frequently used?
   Place a comma before (in front of) a coordinate conjunction when that conjunction joins two independent clauses.
4. What is the *after* comma rule?
   Place a comma after a long introductory clause or phrase.
5. Explain a comma splice; what is it?
   A comma splice is the incorrect use of the comma. The most frequent comma splice error is the placing of the comma between two independent clauses.
6. When following the *before* comma rule, where precisely is the comma written or typed? The comma is typed in the space directly after the last letter of the word immediately in front of the coordinate conjunction.
7. State the *before* comma rule.
   Place a comma before a coordinate conjunction when that conjunction joins two independent clauses.
8. Write the seven coordinate conjunctions we learn from FANBOYS.
   for, and, nor, but, or, yet, so
9. Define a preposition.
   A preposition is a word that joins its object to the rest of the sentence, forming a prepositional phrase.
10. Why is the *after* comma rule called the *after* rule? What is after what?
    The comma is after the long introductory clause or phrase.
11. Define an introductory clause.
    An introductory clause is a dependent clause that appears at the beginning of a sentence. It is called introductory because it introduces an independent clause that follows it.
12. What mark of punctuation can replace the comma and coordinate conjunction that separates two independent clauses?
    The semicolon (;).

13. The comma rule that states, "*long introductory clauses*" refers to the number of words in a dependent clause. What number is long?
    Six or more words is considered long.
14. Define a complex sentence.
    A complex sentence contains only one independent clause and one or more dependent clauses.
15. Did Jerusalem allow begging on its streets?
    Yes
16. Does Atlanta allow begging on its streets?
    No
17. Define a compound sentence.
    A compound sentence contains two or more independent clauses.
18. What do the two "Dear Jack" letters show us?
    They show how the placing of commas can drastically control interpretation.
19. Define a compound-complex sentence.
    A compound-complex sentence contains two or more independent clauses and one or more dependent clauses.
20. Why is comma rule four a "ringer"?
    it covers very many uses of the comma, a multitude *of sins*
21. Define a *nonrestrictive* element.
    A nonrestrictive element is a nonessential element. This is a word or group of words in a sentence that is set off with commas because it is not essential to carry the meaning or thrust of the sentence. *Hodges' Harbrace Handbook* gives the following sentence as an example of the nonrestrictive element, which is italicized and set off with commas (786). Carol Murphy, *president of the university*, plans to meet with alumni representatives.
22. Are *nonrestrictive* words, phrases or dependent clauses set off with commas?
    Yes
23. Define a *restrictive* element.
    A restrictive element is an essential element. Example from *Sacred Grammar*, "Everyone *who walks a mile every day* will live to see her 80th birthday." The restrictive element is italicized and is *not* set off with commas. Were the relative clause removed from this sentence, the message intended is lost. Essential elements do not have commas surrounding them.

24. Are *restrictive* words or phrases set off with commas?
    No
25. Why is *who walks every day* in the example given in this chapter restrictive?
    Who walks every day carries the essential message of the sentence; therefore, no commas are needed.
26. Exodus 34:14 gives God a rather unusual name. What is it?
    Jealous
27. Nonrestrictive elements are often (but not always) signaled by what two pronouns?
    who and which
28. What kind of pronouns are those mentioned in number 27?
    They are relative pronouns
29. Define parenthetical expressions.
    Words, phrases or clauses that add detail to a sentence but are not essential for understanding the core meaning of the sentence. Commas, dashes or parentheses separate these expressions from the rest of the sentences.
30. How do *Sacred Grammar* and *The Thomson Handbook* disagree on the *series* comma rule?
    Sacred Grammar sees no reason to place a comma in front of the *and* when listing words in a series. Example: Bring pencils, notebooks, dictionaries and laptops to the writing retreat. Note that *Sacred Grammar* does not place a comma between *dictionaries* and *and*. *The Thomson Handbook* places a comma between those two words.
31. How does the sixteenth edition of *Hodges' Harbrace Handbook* define appositive?
    "An appositive is a pronoun, noun or noun phrase that identifies, describes, or explains an adjacent pronoun, noun, or noun phrase" (718).
32. How does *The Thomson Handbook* define appositive?
    A word or phrase that functions as a noun equivalent. It restates, renames, or otherwise more fully defines the noun preceding it: "Candice, **an avid golfer,** started playing at 7:00 AM." (G-8).
33. Is a zip code that follows the name of the state in an address set off with commas?
    No

34. Write a sentence that shows the month, day and year of Shakespeare's death.
   William Shakespeare died on April 23, 1616.
35. The made-up word *commaitis* describes what punctuation error?
   Incorrect comma placement, often excessive, unnecessary use of the comma

Self-Quiz for Chapter Eleven: Writing That Paper

1. What rescued Dr. Beaty from being a dull English professor at least in the mind of one student?
   My knowing something about race driver Richard Petty.
2. Exodus 17:14a teaches what about remembering?
   Writing it down helps to remember.
3. Exodus 34:1 tells what happened to the first writing of the Ten Commandments. What happened to the first copy?
   Moses broke the tablets.
4. What necessitated the writing of the book of Deuteronomy?
   People forget.
5. What talent do we know was possessed by at least one of the spies that Joshua sent to survey the promise land?
   One could provide a written description.
6. What is the strange metaphor of Psalm 45:1?
   "My tongue is the pen of a skillful writer."
7. The teachers of the law and the Pharisees wanted to stone the adulterous woman in John 8. What did Rabbi Jesus want to do with her?
   He wanted to protect her.
8. What group of people in John 8 first dropped their stones and left the temple courts?
   The elderly men dropped their rocks and left.
9. What might have Rabbi Jesus written on the ground at the scene of arresting the woman? He may have put into writing what he was about to say, "If any one of you is without sin, let him be the first to throw the first stone at her."
10. Often the message of the metaphor is stronger than what?
    The message of the metaphor is stronger than the metaphor itself.
11. What are the first three items on our "to do" list in writing the essay?

(1) Choose a subject, (2) make a list of ideas, and (3) categorize the list of ideas.
12. Dr. Beaty received a student paper on rap music; what did he do first?
He prayed for deliverance from the snare of the fowler and the pestilence that stalks abroad.
13. What did Dr. Beaty do after he read the paper on rap music?
He acknowledged the paper as worthwhile because he had learned valuable information.
14. The students who botched the Isaiah writing should have started with what in preparation for writing?
A list of ideas
15. State the main difference between the Isaiah students who failed and the Richard Petty scholar who succeeded.
Energy, appetite
16. This chapter mentions three different kinds of outlines; name them.
(1) Sentence outlines, (2) working outlines, and (3) topical outlines.
17. Of the three outlines mentioned in this chapter, *Sacred Grammar* recommends which one for our purposes?
The topical outline
18. What is the significance of the metaphor of the cluster of grapes?
It symbolizes the unity of the paragraph.
19. Sheridan Baker and *Sacred Grammar* ask that the thesis statement appear where in the writing of the essay?
Both ask that the thesis statement be placed as the last sentence of the introductory paragraph.
20. Define concrete image.
A concrete image is a word or piece of information from the outside world or from our bodies that come to our consciousness through one of the five senses.
21. Of the three ways to make transitions from paragraph to paragraph, which is used most? The picking up of an idea from the previous paragraph and introducing it in the first sentence of the new paragraph is used most of the three.
22. What two groups of transitional words work well as the first word in a new paragraph? Conjunctive adverbs and coordinate conjunctions

23. How does the Slinky help the writer improve paragraphs?
    The Slinky's smooth walk down the steps is a model of the way sentences move down the paragraph.
24. Sheridan Baker's opening invitation does what?
    It gets the reader's attention.
25. Paul the Apostle used what transitional word to begin chapter 8 of the book of Romans? The conjunctive adverb *therefore*
26. Who determines the length of the conclusion of a given essay?
    The writer

WORKS CITED

Amar, Ahkil Reed. *America's Constitution: A Biography.* New York: Random House, 2005.

Berrigan, Daniel. *Isaiah: Spirit of Courage, Gift of Tears*. Minneapolis: Fortress Press, 1996.

Blakesley, David and Jeffrey L. Hoogeveen. *The Thomson Handbook.* Boston: Thomson Wadsworth, 2008.

Bloom, Harold. *Genius.* New York: Warner Books, 2002.

Brueggemann, Walter. *Isaiah 1–39*. Louisville: Westminster John Kim Press.

Dickens, Charles. *Little Dorrit*. New York: Meridian Classic, 1986.

Elliott, Rebecca. *Painless Grammar*. Hauppauge, New York: 1997.

Gaston, Thomas E. and Bret H. Smith. *The Research Paper: A Common-Sense Approach*.

Englewood Cliffs, New Jersey: Prentice-Hall, 1988.

Glenn, Cheryl and Loretta Gray. *Hodges' Harbrace Handbook*, 16th Ed. Boston: Thomson Wadsworth, 2007.

Glenn, Cheryl and Robert Keith Miller, Suzanne Strobeck Webb and Loretta Gray. *Hodges' Harbrace Handbook,* 15th Ed. Boston: Thomson Wadsworth, 2004.

Gordon, Karen Elizabeth. *The New Well-Tempered Sentence.* New York: Houghton Mifflin, 1993.

Hairston, Maxine and John J. Ruszkiewicz. *The Scott, Foresman Handbook for Writers,* 2nd Ed. New York: 1991.

Holy Bible New International Version. Grand Rapids, Michigan: Zondervan, 1983.

Kirszner, Laurie G. and Stephen R. Mandell. *The Holt Handbook.* New York: Holt, Rinehart and Winston, 1986.

Lutz, Gary and Diane Stevenson. *The Writer's Digest Grammar Desk Reference.* Cincinnati: Writer's Digest Books, 2006.

O'Conner, Patricia T. *Woe Is I.* New York: Riverhead Books, 2003.

Roth, Audrey J. *The Research Paper: Process, Form and Content,* 6th Ed. Belmont California: Wadsworth Publishing Company, 1989.

Skwire, Sarah E. and David Skwire. *Writing with a Thesis,* 9th Ed. Boston: Thomson Wadsworth, 2005.

Strumpf, Michael and Auriel Douglas. *The Grammar Bible.* New York: Henry Holt and Company, 1999.

Troyka, Lynn Quitman. *Simon & Schuster Handbook for Writers,* 6th Ed. Upper Saddle River, New Jersey, 2002.

Truss, Lynne. *Eats, Shoots & Leaves.* New York: Gotham Books: 2003.

GENERAL INDEX

A

Aaron (brother of Moses), 165
adjectives, 18, 84, 199-200, 206-7. *See also* parts of speech
adverbs, 18. *See also* parts of speech
"after" comma rule, 54, 64, 146, 149, 151
Amalekite Army, 165
Amar, Akhil Reed, 130
  Americas Constitution: A Biography, 130
America's Constitution: A Biography (Amar), 130, 215
appositives, 58
  nonrestrictive, 158
  restrictive, 159
auxiliary verb, 99, 103, 107-9
  modal, 109, 123

B

Baker, Sheridan, 183
Beak of the Finch, The (Weiner), 159
Beaty, Anita, 9, 138
Beaty, Caroline, 30
Beaty, Dawn, 30
Beaty, Elijah, 30

Beaty, Jackson, 30
Beaty, Jim, 30, 138
  Sacred Grammar, 12-14, 164
Beaty, Jordan, 30
Beaty, Wil, 30
"before" comma rule, 143, 146, 149, 151
Berrigan, Daniel
  Isaiah: Spirit of Courage, Gift of Tears, 179, 182
Blakesley, David
  Thompson Handbook, The, 152
Bloom, Harold, 39, 82
Brief English Handbook, The, 134
Brueggemann, Walter, 138
  Isaiah 1–39, 180
Bush, George W., 158

C

case, 24-25, 32, 88
changing word, 37, 40, 43, 46-47
Churchill, Winston, 21, 38
clause, 20, 36, 71, 92
  adverbial, 47
  definition of, 36
  dependent, 26, 46-47, 73, 106-7, 139

independent, 37, 71, 78, 106-7, 139
introductory, 46, 146
relative, 26
clause maker tunnel. *See* parts of
    speech: chart
clause test, 50, 74, 80, 147
    importance of, 82
Colbert, Steven, 216
commaitis, 162, 211
comma rule
    number 1, 143-46, 151
    number 2, 146-50, 151
    number 3, 150-51
    number 4, 151-62
commas
    in dates, 161
    with introductory elements, 159
    in long numbers, 162
    in place names, 161
    with quotations, 160-61
    with transitional expressions, 160
comma splice, 144, 151
complements, 86, 89, 198-99
conclusion, 179-83
concrete image, 66, 212
conjunction, 19. *See also* parts of
    speech
conjunctive adverb, 41, 182
    author's favorite, 66
    frequently used, 58
    list, 65
connector tunnel. *See* parts of speech: chart
Constitution of the United States, 130
coordinate conjunctions, 21, 57-58,
    82, 196, 199, 208, 212
    comma rule of, 74, 143-44, 146,
        151, 156
    using sparingly, 39

D

David (biblical king), 104
Dickens, Charles
    Little Dorrit, 17
direct object, 87, 109
    decorating, 79, 83, 90

E

Eats, Shoots & Leaves (Truss), 149, 216
Elliott, Rebecca
    Painless Grammar, 100
equal sign, 58, 60, 62, 64. *See also*
    semicolon

F

FANBOYS. *See* coordinate
    conjunctions
Fisher, Beaty, 30
Fisher, Trey, 30
fragment, 37

G

gerunds, 131-34. *See also* verbals
Gordon, Karen Elizabeth
    New Well-Tempered Sentence, The, 66
Gospels, synoptic, 15-16
grammar rule, cardinal, 17, 113

H

Hardy, Thomas
    "Neutral Tones," 120
Hebrew Bible
    infinitives in, 140
    present perfect verbs in, 99

simple sentences in, 37-38
Hodges' Harbrace Handbook
   on cases, 24-25
   on comma and conjunctive adverbs, 65
   list of subordinate conjunctions, 66
   on past perfect tense, 97
   on present perfect tense, 99
Hoogeveen, Jeffrey L.
   Thompson Handbook, The, 152, 215
Hopkins, Gerard Manly
   "Windhover, The," 121
horizontal approach, 20
Hur (companion of Moses), 165

I

indirect objects, 32, 88
   decorating, 83, 86
infinitive phrase, 139-40
infinitives, 47, 138-41. *See also* verbals
interjection, 19-20. *See also* parts of speech
interrupters, 159
Isaiah 1–39 (Brueggemann), 180
Isaiah: Spirit of Courage, Gift of Tears (Berrigan), 182

J

Jesus, 30, 32, 34, 49, 75, 81

K

King, Martin Luther, Jr., 39, 82

L

Little Dorrit (Dickens), 17, 215

M

"Magnificat, The," 61
modifier tunnel. *See* parts of speech: chart
Moses, 30, 32, 104, 165

N

NASCAR (National Association for Stock Car Auto Racing), 13
"Neutral Tones" (Hardy), 120
New Well-Tempered Sentence, The (Gordon), 66, 215
NIV (New International Version), 13, 28, 31, 45, 49, 59, 61, 72, 75, 136, 147, 216
   and and *but* in, 75
   commas in, 61
nonrestrictive dependent clause, 154-56
nonrestrictive elements, 151-56, 158
nonrestrictive participial phrase, 155
nouns, 16-17. *See also* parts of speech
NRSV (New Revised Standard Version), 157, 169

O

objective case, 27, 32
object territory, 25
O'Conner, Patricia T.
   Woe Is I, 92
O'Dowd, McIver, 30
O'Dowd, Whitner, 30

P

Painless Grammar (Elliott), 100, 215
parenthetical expressions, 157
participial phrase, 137, 155

participles, 138. *See also* verbals
parts of speech, 12, 20
   chart, 20
   See also individual parts of speech
Paul, Saint (the apostle), 24, 39, 65, 183
Peter (the apostle), 27-28, 147-48
Petty, Richard, 13-14
phrase, 21
   decorating, 79-81, 90
   definition, 81
possessive case, 25
   plural, 31-32
   power in, 34
   singular, 28-30
predicate, 36, 105
predicate adjective, 87-90
predicate complement, 105
predicate noun, 86-87, 105
preposition, 19, 33, 133, 145
   of Churchill, 21
   object of, 22
   See also parts of speech
pronoun complements, 89
pronouns
   indefinite, 25
   personal, 25
   reflexive, 25
   relative, 26, 35, 55, 68
Publication Manual of the American Psychological Association, The, 125

R

restrictive element, 152-53

S

Sacred Grammar (Beaty), 12, 14, 164
Sanhedrin, 27, 121

SAT (Scholastic Assessment Test), 26
semicolon, 58, 60, 62-64, 66. *See also* equal sign
sentence
   complex, 43-55
   compound, 57-69
   compound-complex, 71-77
   simple, 36-41, 71
sentence decorating, 90
sentence diagramming, 79
sentence structure, 59, 63, 149
Shakespeare, William, 39
Simon and Schuster Handbook for Writers, 58, 99
Smoltz, John, 15
Song of Mary. *See* "Magnificat, The"
Song of Moses, 167
speech, parts of. *See* parts of speech
subject, 24
   compound, 38-39, 127, 202
subjective case, 24, 27, 32-33, 204
   examples, 88-89
subject territory, 25
subject-verb agreement, 112-13
subject-verb cluster, 20
subordinate clause, 35, 54
subordinate conjunctions, 21, 43-46, 66-67
subordination, 43, 50, 67, 85. *See also* subordinate conjunctions

T

Ten Commandments, 211
Thompson Handbook, The (Blakesley and Hoogeveen), 152
transitional phrase, 66
Truss, Lynne
   Eats, Shoots & Leaves, 149

V

verbals, 141. *See also* gerunds; infinitives; participles
verb moods
  imperative, 121, 122
  indicative, 121
  subjunctive, 122-23
verbs, 18
  to be, 101-3
  intransitive, 87-88, 110
  irregular, 107, 112, 115-20
  linking, 88-89, 108
  main, 99, 103, 107
  regular, 97, 112-15
  transitive, 87, 105, 109-10
  voices of, 124-26
  See also parts of speech

verb tenses, 94, 106
  future perfect, 102-3
  future tense, 94-95, 131
  past perfect, 98, 100, 102-3
  present perfect, 95-97, 99-100, 102
  regular present, 112-14
  regular progressive, 131
vertical approach, 20

W

Weiner, Jonathan
  Beak of the Finch, The, 159
White, E. B., 39
Whitman, Walt, 62
"Windhover, The" (Hopkins), 121
Woe Is I (O'Conner), 92, 216
writers, biblical, 165-66

SCRIPTURE INDEX

A

Acts
  1:3, 33-34
  1:5, 144
  2:1, 147
  2:32, 145-46
  2:43, 146
  3:4, 148
  3:11, 147-48
  3:16a, 149
  3:16b, 132
  3:17a, 106
  3:19, 132
  4:12, 145
  5, 27
  5:15b, 25
  5:30, 28
  5:32, 26
  7:20, 125
  17:16, 19
  18:8a, 158
  20:24a, 40
  27:27-44, 76
  27:39, 76-77
Amos
  5:11a, 38

C

Colossians
  2:15, 24

D

Daniel
  1:5a, 108
  2:21, 84
  4:12b, 144
  8:8, 124
Deuteronomy
  6:4-9, 165
  6:9, 165
  17, 166
  17:18, 166
  27:2-3, 167
  27:8, 167
  28:7, 107
  31:19, 167
  32:1-43, 167
  32:24, 135

E

Ecclesiastes
  4:1b, 84

10:15, 160
Ephesians
  1:3, 19
  1:4a, 39-40
Exodus
  9:10, 16
  14:19, 155
  16:27, 157
  17:14a, 165
  19:3, 18
  19:4, 18, 93-94
  20:18b, 160
  21:12, 153
  22:3, 107
  24:17, 135
  29:23, 160
  33:5, 123
  34:1, 165
  34:14, 156
Ezekiel
  14:14, 125
  28:13, 151

F

1 Corinthians
  2:9b, 153
  7:29, 90
  14:40, 13
1 John
  4:17a, 126
1 Kings
  3:1a, 18
  8:42, 111
  17:1a, 127, 202
  17:14a, 114
  18, 74
  18:2b, 74
1 Samuel

11:5, 90

G

Galatians
  3:26, 95
  4:14, 123
  5:21b, 95
  5:24, 106
  6:7b, 106
Genesis
  1:1, 21, 95
  1:1a, 22
  1:3, 40
  1:6, 40
  1:9, 40
  1:14, 40
  1:20, 40
  1:24, 40
  3:12, 86
  6:7, 160
  6:9b, 154, 156
  7:4, 107
  9:25, 160
  11:10b, 154, 156
  12:7b, 154, 156
  14:19, 156
  17:8, 155-56
  18:6b, 160
  19:3b, 155
  21:16, 111
  27:20b, 158
  30:42, 123
  31:7b, 159
  31:54, 101

H

Habakuk

2:2, 109
Hebrews
  4, 17
  5:6, 44
  8:10b, 171
  10:15-16, 171
  11:23, 32
  11:24, 32

I

Isaiah
  1:1-18, 173-74, 177
  1:1a, 136
  1:4a, 136
  1:5, 137
  1:5b, 137
  1:6b, 137
  1:7, 177
  1:10, 177
  1:11, 177
  1:15, 177
  1:17, 177
  1:17a, 177
  1:17b, 177
  1:18, 172, 177-78
  1:18-20, 177
  6:9, 62
  7:21, 157
  7:23, 157
  12:5, 110
  23:16, 110
  48:18, 109
  49:16a, 128, 204
  62:6a, 36
  64:4, 153

J

Jeremiah
  3:7, 72
  5:11, 37-38
  7:2, 139
  7:10, 139
  7:10b, 139
  7:18, 139-40
  7:18b, 140
  7:31, 139-40
  7:31a, 140
  7:33, 139-40
  7:33b, 140
  8:20, 121
  11:14b, 109
  13:10, 44
  26:9b, 21
  27:18a, 108
  33:6, 157
  36, 168-69
  36:22-26, 168
  36:27-32, 169
  36:32b, 169
  44:24, 153
Job
  28:7, 97
  32:6, 108
  40:4a, 108
Joel
  2:9, 114
  2:23, 111
John
  1:3, 126
  1:3a, 126
  3:16, 68-69, 112, 149
  4:43, 40

8:7b, 171
9:28a, 85
10:13, 113
11:35, 37, 44, 48, 73, 79-80, 110
13:1, 32-34
13:1b, 106
13:18, 104
13:19, 104
18:5, 105
18:6, 105
18:12b, 107
18:14a, 107
19:12, 153
19:21, 171
20:20b, 33
Jonah
  3:3a, 110
Joshua
  18:4, 168
Judges
  7:21, 135
  8:27, 43
  14:17, 16
  16:18, 111

L

Lamentations
  2:7, 99
Leviticus
  7:16, 133
Luke
  1:3-4, 170
  1:46-55, 62
  1:51, 60-61
  2:9, 59
  2:25b, 59-60
  2:29-32, 60
  4:22a, 81

8:10b, 62, 171
9:54, 159
12:49, 123
20:40, 81-82

M

Mark
  1:10, 45-49, 51
  1:14, 48-49, 51
  1:22, 49-51
  1:29, 50
  1:35, 52
  3:13, 93-94
  6:2b, 96
  7:32, 75
  10:9, 53
  10:10, 53
  10:12, 53
  10:14, 53
  10:17, 54
  10:22b, 54
  10:31, 75
  10:38a, 54
  11:21, 19
  12:17a, 122
  13:38a, 122
  14:37, 121
  14:61, 121
Matthew
  2:19b, 28
  3:4a, 28
  5:34b, 28
  7:5b, 28
  9:9a, 29
  9:10, 29
  9:14, 29
  9:23, 29
  10:41, 29

11:7a, 29
11:8, 31
12:29a, 29
12:42b, 29
13:27a, 29
13:55, 29
14:3b, 29
14:6a, 29
14:12a, 29
15:27, 31
15:22, 135
16:27a, 29
18:26a, 29
21:25, 29
22:16b, 124
22:17, 124
22:21, 29
23:1, 29, 31, 110
23:2, 29-32, 96
23:4, 31
23:13, 31
23:22, 29
23:23, 96
23:27, 31
23:27b, 32
26:51, 29-30
27:7, 29
27:9, 29
27:15, 29
27:24, 29
27:27, 29
27:37, 158
27:56, 29
27:58, 29-30
28:6a, 107
Micah
  6:8, 140

N

Nahum
  2:10, 108
Numbers
  14:4, 109
  24:3, 111

P

Philippians
  4:7, 93
Psalms
  2:11, 133
  12:5, 133
  29:4, 90
  31:10, 133
  41:9, 104
  45:1b, 169
  55:16b, 112
  55:17b, 112
  55:18a, 112
  55:20a, 113
  131:2a, 109
  135:3, 90

R

Revelation
  7:17, 40
  19:3, 160
  21, 94
  21:5b-7, 95
Romans
  1:7, 124
  4:2, 160
  7:25b, 183
  15:18, 97
  16:4, 90

S

2 Corinthians
　11:31, 153
　13:5b, 157
2 John
　1:8b, 126
2 Kings
　1:13a, 83-84
　17:4, 125
2 Samuel
　15:18b, 45
　17:29b, 108
　18:18b, 17
　19:32a, 18

2 Timothy
　2:15, 13
　4:6, 19
Song of Solomon
　2:16, 62

T

3 John
　1:5, 90

Z

Zephaniah
　2:5, 158

Printed in Great Britain
by Amazon.co.uk, Ltd.,
Marston Gate.